Maw Broon's
Remedies An' Suchlike
(My wee book o' bits an' pieces)

Waverley Books

Published 2009 by Waverley Books Ltd, David Dale House, New Lanark,
Scotland, ML11 9DJ

Produced by Waverley Books Ltd, with selected Health and Beauty text
first published 1930 in Everything Within - published by News Chronicle
and George Newnes Ltd, London, © 2009 IPC + Syndication, with additional
material by the Waverley Books team.
Design and layout by Hugo Breingan

ISBN: 978-1-902407-95-1

Printed and bound in the EU

WARNING !

The material contained in this book is set out in good faith for general
guidance and interest only. Whilst every effort has been made to ensure that
the information in this book is accurate, this book is sold on the condition
that neither the authors nor the publisher can be found legally responsible
for the consequences of any errors or omissions.

Diagnosis and treatment are skilled undertakings which must always
be carried out by a doctor and not from the pages of a book.
Do not undertake any course of treatment without the advice of your doctor.
Never stop taking medication without the agreement of your doctor.

Some essential oils, when used inappropriately can be highly toxic.
Some essential oils are unsuitable for use at home.
Consult a professional aromatherapist before undertaking any course
of treatment with essential oils.
Do not use essential oils in pregnancy, or on babies and young children,
without the advice of a trained aromatherapist.
Some medical conditions contraindicate the use of certain
essential oils and/or massage.
Do not ingest essential oils or use essential oils in the eyes.
Do not use essential oils undiluted on the skin unless otherwise indicated.
If using homeopathy or herbal medicine in conjunction with aromatherapy, seek the
advice of the relevant practitioner as well as the aromatherapist.

Remedies & Suchlike

This first bit is actually my ain Mither's notebook — she gave me it when I was a lass — and that wisnae the day, nor yesterday!

It's a' still there — she was awfy keen that I looked after m'sel' a bit better, but I didn't really look at it too much till I had my ain family. I've added to it, but I think Daphne and Maggie have had mair use o' it than me — and we've a' had a bit o' a smile at some o' the auld-fashioned ideas about health and makin' yersel' beautiful.

You'll find at the end o' this auld bit, my copy o' the fund-raiser that the 'afternoon tea ladies' did for 'The School'. It's pretty well up to date about stains and suchlike.

Maw

Dear Margaret,

I can't believe how quickly you have grown up. Quite the young lady. But oh – so headstrong.

I really wish you wouldn't spend so much time with that family. The young man is – well – he's going to be a common tradesman! I saw him with a toolbag and filthy dungarees!

I think it is time to pass to you my book of pointers and beauty tips, in the hope that you will start to think a little more carefully about your future, so that you can find someone rather more suitable. You need to take more care about your posture and start to think about lady-like things.

More time indoors please, and less time with The Broons. (I take it that their proper name is Brown?)

You have your reputation to think about and with a little work, and deft make-up, you can be a great catch for someone taller, darker and rather more handsome than that Broon boy.

As for his father – I am sure he's the one that whistles at me as I pass that allotment. He seems most familiar.

Your loving Mother

Acne. Girls between 16 and 20 years of age often suffer from various small pimples which come and go, occasionally leaving little scars. Generally these pimples appear chiefly on the chin and forehead, but occasionally they are found only on the nose, giving a red nose, which is very unbecoming. These pimples are called acne, and diet plays a very large part in the cure. Sweets and rich cakes and pastries should be avoided. Fruit, especially fresh fruit, ought to replace sweets, and plenty of green vegetables and salads eaten. It is also advisable to take a dose of saline salts every morning and to drink at least a quart of water daily, taking it in small quantities between meals.

For outward application a lotion made of 1 drachm of sulphate of zinc, 1 drachm of sulpho-carbolate of potassium, and 4 oz of rosewater will be found very beneficial. It should be dabbed over the affected parts with a pad of cotton-wool twice daily. The skin should be washed with warm water and a lather of good soap, and dried before the lotion is applied.

Drachm —
a drachm is a unit of capacity or volume in the old apothecary system equal to one eighth of a fluid ounce which equals 3.75 ml (³/₄ of a teaspoon).

Adhesive Plasters. These are often used in the treatment of wrinkles, especially the "frowning" wrinkles which form between the eyebrows. The plasters are cut from pieces of sticking-plaster in the shape required; and, after the skin has been bathed with warm water to soften it, the plaster is fixed over the wrinkle and allowed to remain on as long as possible.

For frowning wrinkles, cut the plaster in a three-cornered shape, placing it with the pointed portion towards the bridge of the nose. For "crows-feet", cut a crescent-shaped piece, and for lines from nose to mouth, straight strips. This method of treating wrinkles is more successful in the case of frowning wrinkles than with "crows-feet" or nose to mouth lines. The

ADHESIVE
PLASTERS?
OOR DAPHNE
USES DUCT TAPE!

plaster should be worn at night and during the day when reading or working. It is a great help to those who are in the habit of wrinkling the brows when their thoughts are concentrated.

Alopecia. or baldness in patches, is, in the majority of cases, due to conditions of the nervous system. An iron tonic invariably helps and occasionally electrical treatment is beneficial. A lotion consisting of 2 drachms of vinegar of cantharides to 2 oz. of rectified spirit, dabbed over the scalp daily with a pad of cotton-wool will, in many instances, effect a cure.

Ankles. Slender ankles are considered desirable. To reduce an ankle that is too thick, dissolve ½ an oz. of Epsom salts in a foot-bath of hot water. Soak the feet in this, allowing the water to come well up over the ankles, for at least fifteen minutes, keeping the water at the same temperature all the time by adding fresh as the water in the bath cools.

Dry the feet and ankles, and massage with a few drops of extract of witch-hazel, rubbing firmly from the instep towards the calf of the leg. When massaging the back of the ankle use the thumb and second finger, grasping the ankle firmly and pinching and kneading the flesh. Give the treatment every night, and sleep with a bandage fixed firmly, but not too tightly, around the ankle.

Ankles that are inclined to swell should be painted with colourless iodine and a pillow placed at the foot of the bed, so that the feet may be slightly raised during sleep. This will be very helpful in keeping the swelling down.

6

<u>Three Exercises for Reducing the Ankles.</u> 1. Sit on a low chair and extend the leg with the foot straight out, toes pointing downwards. Rotate the foot round and round, moving it from the ankle. Exercise first one foot then the other, keeping up the exercise for about ten minutes night and morning.

2. Draw an imaginary straight line across the room and, rising on the toes, walk along it, lowering the foot to the heel and rising again on the toes at each step.

3. Stand erect, raise one foot from the floor, throwing the weight of the body on the other. Stretch the raised foot out in front and shake it out loosely from the ankle. Treat the other in the same way, repeating the exercise five to ten times with each foot.

<u>Arms.—To Whiten.</u> Take 2 oz. of distilled rosewater and add to them 1 teaspoonful each of strained lemon juice and peroxide of hydrogen (10 vols.). Shake well and, with a pad of cotton-wool, dab over the arms. Allow to dry on and then rub the skin over lightly with fine oatmeal. Do this in the morning and at night. Rub some cold cream into the arms after washing and drying them.

<u>For Arms that are too Thin.</u> If the arms are too thin, practise the following exercises every morning from ten to twenty times each:

1. Extend the arms straight in front, on a level with the shoulders. Take a deep breath, clench the fists, and bring the arms to the shoulders. Extend them again and bring them once more to the shoulders. Exhale and repeat.

2. Take a deep breath, raise the arms and extend them horizontally with the shoulders. Clench the hands and touch the shoulders with the clenched fists. Extend them again and repeat. When practising these exercises remember to keep the muscles of the arms and shoulders as rigid as possible.

<u>The Too-plump Arm.</u> To reduce the too-plump arm, massage every night and morning with a mixture of one part spirits of camphor and

three parts orangeflower water. First bathe the arms, then massage, using the lotion in place of a cream and working from the wrists towards the elbows and from the elbows towards the shoulders.

Rough, Red Arms will be much improved if gently massaged with cold cream at night and dabbed with calamine lotion in the morning. Any chemist will supply a bottle of calamine lotion.

When the backs of the arms are rough and red, squeeze a loofah out in warm water, soap it thickly, and rub the arms briskly, but not too roughly with it. Rinse off the soap, dry, and apply a little cold cream, rubbing it in very thoroughly. Then dust with fine oatmeal.

Astringents. For a greasy skin the use of a mild astringent lotion, after cleansing the face with cream and before applying any form of "make up," is essential if blackheads and enlarged pores are to be avoided. Camphor water, to which simple tincture of benzoin has been added in the proportion of 15 drops of the benzoin to every ounce of the water, makes a mild astringent which also has a whitening effect on the skin.

A stronger astringent can be made by mixing together 1 oz. of eau de Cologne, 2 oz. of extract of witch-hazel, and 4 oz. of distilled rosewater. When mixed, add 50 drops of simple tincture of benzoin. Only the very mildest astringent should be used on a dry skin, and then after the face has been well massaged with cream.

Astringents should always be applied as cold as possible. Stand the bottle in cold water before use if no ice-box is available. The effect on the pores and muscles of the face is greater when the lotion is applied cold.

Back, Beauty for the In these days of the backless evening frock, not to mention the sunbathing costume, a straight, supple back is an invaluable possession. If the back is too thin the bones will show, the shoulder blades appear prominent, and the effect will be far from attractive. The too-thin back can be made plumper by massage with a little feeding cream.

It is not, however, possible to massage the back successfully oneself, and the services of a maid or friend must be secured. A little of the cream should be placed in the palm of the hand and well rubbed in, with a circular movement, rubbing round and round, and working from just above the waistline to the base of the neck.

The Too-plump Back. When the back is too plump, and ridges of fat form just below the shoulder blades and at the base of the neck, the effect is both ugly and ageing. Hard, firm massage is necessary in this case. The hands should be dusted with talcum powder and the patient should lie flat on her face. The back is massaged very firmly, pinching and kneading the unwanted flesh vigorously. Ten to fifteen minutes' massage, given every day, should effect a great improvement in a few weeks.

Backache. Although not exactly a beauty subject, backache can spoil one's general appearance, for the back that aches will surely sag, and a sagging spine leads to round shoulders and an ungraceful carriage.

If the back aches habitually, take an iron tonic and make a rule of lying flat on the back for at least half an hour a day. Do not lie on a bed or sofa. The floor, with a rug spread on it, is best, or if a draught is feared, lie on a table. No pillow should be used.

Herbs at Home

Lavender

Lavender
(Lavandula vera or L. officinalis) Family: Lamiaceae (Labiateae)
The essential oil is obtained by steam distillation from the flowers of the plant.
Origins/History: Lavender is indigenous to mountainous regions of the western Mediterranean and widely cultivated in Britain. In days gone by it was used as a condiment and flavouring, and as a furniture

Burnett's Herbal Teas
"Nature's Wonders"

Baths, Beauty. A daily bath is essential to a clear, beautiful skin. The water should be between 95° and 98° F.

Whit? A bath every day! Once a month mair like if we can get awa' wi' it!

9

Baths for the Too Stout. Dissolve from 2 to 4 oz. of Epsom salts in a bath, letting the water be as hot as can be comfortably borne. Remain in the bath for from ten to fifteen minutes, keeping the water at the same temperature by adding more as the water in the bath cools.

A brisk massage should be given with a rough towel after the bath, special attention being given to any portions of the body which are most in need of reducing. These reducing baths should be taken at night, and the "patient" should retire to bed immediately afterwards.

Baths for the Too Thin. The girl who is too thin about the neck, shoulders, etc., will find a sage-and-lavender bath beneficial. Two tablespoonfuls of sage leaves (fresh, if possible; if not, the dried leaves may be used) should be placed in a butter-muslin bag with a dessertspoonful of lavender tops and a few pieces of dried orange peel. Put the bag in a quart of boiling water and leave to soak till the water is quite cold. Squeeze out and add to the bath.

A Bran-and-Lemon Bath. To soften and whiten the skin and help to reduce enlarged pores, there is nothing better than a bran-and-lemon bath. Put three tablespoonfuls of bran and a teaspoonful of dried and shredded lemon peel in a bag of butter-muslin. Place the bag in boiling water and allow to soak for fifteen minutes. Squeeze out the bag and add the water to the bath.

A Steam Bath for the Face. To clear the complexion, whiten the skin, and remove all impurities, give the face a steam bath. Put a tablespoonful of flowers of sulphur in a small basin and mix to a thin paste with warm water. Pour a quart of boiling water into a wash-basin and add the flowers of sulphur.

After tying a folded handkerchief across the eyes, to keep the steam from them, hold the head over the basin, throwing a towel over both head and basin to keep the steam in. When the skin feels soft and moist, lather the face with a good soap. Rinse off with clear warm water, and dry lightly.

Next give a second steaming, using fresh boiling water and adding to this second bath a teaspoonful of simple tincture of benzoin. Steam the face over this for three minutes, sponge with cold soft water, and apply a little massage cream.

The Good Neighbour

Bathing & Showering with Essential Oils

Add a few drops (5-10) of essential oil to the bath water after the water has been drawn, then close the door to retain the aromatic vapour. The choice of oils is entirely up to the individual, depending on the desired effect, although those with sensitive skins are advised to have the oils ready diluted in a base oil prior to bathing.

Bathing in essential oils can stimulate and revive or relax and sedate depending on the oils selected : rosemary and pine can have a soothing effect on tired or aching limbs, camomile and lavender are popular for relieving insomnia and anxiety etc.

A similar effect (although obviously not quite as relaxing) can be achieved whilst showering by soaking a wet sponge in essential oil mix, then rubbing it over the body under a warm spray.

Sea Bathing. When sea bathing remember that from fifteen to twenty minutes is long enough for the first bathe of the season. Never bathe immediately after a meal. It is extremely bad for the digestion, and might have serious consequences. Never bathe when very hot after a long walk. The shock of the water on the over-heated skin is most injurious. Never stay in the water once you feel chilly. Do not bathe on an empty stomach. If bathing before breakfast, take some tea and biscuits. Sea salt can be obtained from chemists in cartons, and a salt bath taken in one's own bathroom for a very trifling expenditure. It will be found refreshing and stimulating.

Turkish Baths. A Turkish bath is often very beneficial to those who would lose weight, but one should not be taken without medical advice, for if the heart is not strong it may easily do more harm than good.

In most large towns there are premises with the necessary equipment, where Turkish baths can be obtained, but there are also small cabinets which may be used at home for much the same purpose.

A Rejuvenating Bath. Mix together 4 ounces of surgical spirit, 1 oz. of spirits of ammonia, and 1 oz. of spirits of camphor. Dissolve 2 oz. of sea salt in 1 pint of boiling water and add to the mixed spirits. Shake well and cork tightly. Two tablespoonfuls of this mixture, added to a bath of hot water, is very refreshing and rejuvenating.

Perfumed Bath Bags. To make bath bags to soften and perfume the water, mix together 5 oz. of fine oatmeal, 1 oz. of powdered orris root, 1 oz. of almond meal, and 1½ oz. of Castile soap, finely powdered.

Make some little bags of cheese-cloth, about 4 in. square, fill with the mixture, and tie at the mouth like a miller's sack. One bag will soften and perfume a bath; and the bag can, after being squeezed out, be used as a bath-glove.

Bath Salts. To make bath salts or crystals at home, get 2 lb. of sodium bicarbonate, 1 drachm of oil of lavender, and half a drachm of oil of geranium. Mix the oils together, shaking thoroughly. Take a large jar, with a well-fitted cover and a wide mouth. Put a layer of the sodium about 2 in. deep at the bottom and sprinkle over it half a teaspoonful of the mixed oils. Put another layer of the sodium and another teaspoonful of the oils, repeating the process till the jar is full. Shake well and leave for two or three weeks. If coloured salts are desired, a few drops of cochineal may be added. One tablespoonful should be added to a bath.

Bath Tablets. To make bath tablets at home, take 4 oz. of bicarbonate of soda and 1½ oz. of tartaric acid. Mix together. Mix a drachm of oil of lemon with 5 drops of rose oil (or any scent preferred), and stir them into an ounce of powdered orris root. Add to the tartaric acid and powdered orris root and mix into a stiff paste with a little surgical spirits. Divide into inch-square tablets and place on a baking-sheet to dry. Two tablets will be required to scent and soften the water of a bath.

Herbs at Home

Camomile

Camomile is frequently spelt camomile. The early herbalists used it to cure cases of fluid retention and jaundice. It was also used to treat menstrual pain, painful joints and asthma. It was thought to reduce fevers, cure insomnia and stimulate the appetite.

It was used as sedative in nervous disorders. Externally, it was used to soothe rashes and bruises, to heal sores and to reduce inflammation.

Burnett's Herbal Teas
"Nature's Wonders"

Beauty Beverages.—Barley Water. For a coarse,

blotchy skin there is no better remedy than barley water taken regularly. At least a quart should be consumed every day, and it is best to drink it, half a pint at a time, between meals.

To make barley water, put 1 oz. of pearl barley, after well washing it, into a saucepan with a quart of boiling water, and simmer slowly for an hour. A piece of lemon peel should be added after the water has simmered for half an hour. Allow to become cool, and sweeten to taste.

Sage Tea is another beauty beverage which is excellent for the woman who is too thin and wishes to fill out her arms and the hollows in her neck. Fresh or dried sage leaves may be used.

Place 2 tablespoonfuls of the leaves in a clean teapot and pour over them a pint of boiling water. Allow to stand for five minutes. Strain off, and add a squeeze of orange juice to flavour. A cupful should be taken once or twice daily.

Ooh La La!

Camomile Tea. A most popular beauty beverage amongst French women, and one which is wonderful for making the complexion clear and smooth. Put a tablespoonful of the flowers in a teapot and pour over them a pint of boiling water. Allow to stand for three minutes, strain off, and sweeten to taste. Camomile tea should be taken the last thing at night. Sugar may be omitted if desired.

Beauty Foods.—Apples are amongst the finest beauty foods. If "an apple a day keeps the doctor away," it also wards off blotches and all other forms of complexion blemishes. To obtain the best results, one apple should be taken fasting, before breakfast, and another just before going to bed.

Tomatoes. If the eyes appear dull and the whites are not as clear as you might wish, take a raw tomato with your

FOOD:
Carrots

In folk medicine carrots were used from very early times and for various conditions. They were traditionally considered to be aids to sharp eyesight and were thought to be helpful in regulating the circulation. They were also thought to regulate the menstrual cycle and increase the flow of milk in nursing mothers. Carrots were also taken in the belief that they would act as an appetite stimulant and be effective in a number of disorders associated with the digestive system. They were used to treat flatulence, colic, ulcers, constipation, diarrhoea and haemorhoids. Externally carrots were used, sometimes in a poultice, to speed up the healing of wounds, ulcers, boils and styes. They were also used to treat eczema and chilblains.

breakfast. Do not add pepper or salt, for either of these reduces the beneficial effects of the tomato best taken sliced.

Carrots. Those who are too pale and would like a little natural colour in the cheeks should eat a few raw carrots every day. Choose young soft carrots, scrape them, and cut into very thin slices and eat as sandwiches between thin slices of brown bread and butter. A little cream cheese spread over the carrot will make the sandwich more tasty, and cream cheese is also one of the greatest beauty foods.

Lettuce is a blood purifier and is excellent for those who suffer with spots and blotches. Do not add either vinegar or mayonnaise. A few drops of lemon juice added to the olive oil is sufficient dressing.

SERIES 2

Dr.

FARQUHARSON'S

HERBAL HOME CURES

Cabbage

In ancient Rome cabbage was thought of as being a sovereign remedy that was useful for most things.

In folk medicine it was used as a tonic and in the treatment of stomach disorders, as well as for purifying the blood and cleansing the system. It was thought to have diuretic properties and was used in the treatment of arthritis.

Ulcers were thought to be healed by it, as was heartburn. It was considered to have antiseptic properties and was used to protect against respiratory infections.

In early times raw cabbage was taken to cure nervous complaints. It was also used in some liver conditions and was used to treat alcoholics and as a hangover cure.

Externally, cabbage was used to soothe, cleanse and heal the skin. It was used in the treatment of stings, burns, blisters, ulcers and sores. In the form of poultices, cabbage was used to bring boils to a head, to soothe chest infections and to bring relief to inflamed joints.

Watercress. Watercress is an easy way of taking iron, and those who are in need of a tonic cannot do better than take a little watercress with one or two meals daily. It is also said that watercress is an antidote to the excessive use of tobacco.

Radishes. The woman with a thin, fine skin which wrinkles early in life should try taking radishes for breakfast and tea for removing them. For the little, fine lines around the eyes and mouth, these vegetables are excellent, and unless the wrinkles are very deep, five or six weeks will show a great improvement.

Blackheads. When the skin is coarse and greasy and blackheads are noticed, the amount of greasy, fatty foods should be reduced and plenty of green vegetables, fresh fruit, and salads taken. A glass of water, hot or cold, ought to be drunk first thing in the morning, and another at bedtime.

For external application a mixture of 1 drachm each of oxide of zinc and carbonate of magnesia, and 4 oz. of rosewater is very effective. Mop the lotion over the blackheads and allow to remain on the skin for a short time. Then bathe the face with hot water, and with the corner of a towel passed over the finger, gently press out the blackheads. A little cold cream should be applied when the blackheads have been removed.

An astringent lotion ought always to be used before applying cream or powder for making up by those who are inclined to a coarse skin and blackheads, and all traces of the preparations used during the day removed before sleep. A good cleansing cream or hot water and soap may be used, whichever is preferred. An occasional steam bath is beneficial.

<u>Boils.</u> A boil, however small, can be a great destroyer of beauty. In its early stages a boil may often be dispersed by applying a soap plaster. Moisten a cake of soap and scrape a little of the moist soap off. Place this over the boil, keeping it fixed by means of a piece of sticking-plaster. Do this at night, and often the boil will have disappeared by the morning.

Diet must be carefully studied by all those inclined to boils. Meat should be restricted to the smallest amount and the quantity of sugar and sweets reduced. An iron tonic is advisable when there is a succession of boils, which generally shows an impaired condition in general health.

<u>Brow, Beauty for.</u> A smooth, white forehead contributes very greatly to a girl's attractiveness. To make and keep the brow white and smooth it should be massaged with a good cold cream, smoothing from the eyebrows towards the roots of the hair.

When the pores have absorbed as much of the cream as they can, it should be wiped off with a soft towel and the skin tapped over with a small bag filled with damp salt. The eyes should be kept closed while the salt massage is given, and when the treatment is over the forehead lightly dusted with fine oatmeal. Two or three times a week is often enough for this treatment.

<u>Bunion.</u> The cause of a bunion is generally a badly fitted shoe. The thickening and inflammation can often be reduced by painting with tincture of iodine, and a bandage should be worn at night. If these remedies do not effect relief, a doctor or chiropodist ought to be consulted.

Bust, to Develop. To develop the bust, bathe the chest with warm water and massage with pure olive oil. Put a few drops of the oil in the palm of the hand and work it into the bust, rubbing in an upward and outward direction. Do this at night and in the morning, sponge the chest with very cold water for several minutes.

A teaspoonful of pure olive oil taken after each meal will also help, and breathing exercises are to be recommended. Swimming is particularly beneficial.

Olive Oil

Olive oil had a variety of uses in folk medicine. It was used in the treatment of digestive problems such as flatulence, heartburn, indigestion, ulcers and constipation.

Respiratory problems, such as catarrh and dry coughs, were also treated by it.

Externally it was used to soothe the skin and to relieve the effects of eczema, cold sores and chapped skin. Often with the addition of garlic, it was used as a liniment for sprains or rheumatism. Warm olive oil, sometimes with the addition of a herb such as garlic, was dropped in the ear as a remedy for earache.

An infusion of the leaves of the olive tree was used for cleaning wounds or cuts and was also used as a mouthwash to cure bleeding gums.

Breathing Exercises. 1. Stand erect before an open window, take a deep breath, and extend the arms straight in front, the palms of the hands touching. Spread the arms outwards with a wide sweep, carrying them as far back as possible. Rest, and repeat.

2. Take a light cane, grasp it with both hands and hold it in front level with the waist. With a slow, sweeping movement pass it over the head and down the back as far as can be reached. Rest, and repeat.

Bust, to Reduce. To reduce an over-developed bust, wear a rubber bust bodice over a thin woollen vest, and reduce the amount of liquid taken. A well-fitted brassière will often make an actual reduction unnecessary if worn regularly.

Camomile Flowers. Fair hair that is losing its bright tints can be given pretty golden lights by rinsing with a camomile lotion. First thoroughly shampoo the hair and rinse it in two separate waters. Put 2 oz. of camomile flowers in a large jug, pour over them a pint of boiling water and stir. Cover the jug and allow to stand for 15 minutes. Strain off and use as a last rinse, pouring the liquid over the head again and again.

Dry by rubbing with a warm towel and follow with a good brushing, smearing the brush with a few drops of golden brilliantine.

Fair hair that has turned grey requires a stronger camomile application. For this put 4 oz. of the flowers in an iron saucepan with a quart of boiling water and simmer slowly till the liquid is reduced to half and is the colour of black coffee. Strain off and apply to the hair, allowing it to dry on. Brush, as after the camomile rinse, applying plenty of golden brilliantine, for the camomile application dries the hair.

Carriage. A graceful carriage is a great asset to any woman. Even if her features are plain and her colouring nondescript, with a good walk and an elegant carriage she can command admiration. In Victorian days the greatest attention was paid to what was then termed "deportment" both in school and at home. To-day games have very largely taken the place of deportment. Our girls are healthier, and possibly happier, but their general deportment has not much improved. Slouching is more general, and though they walk more they do not walk so gracefully.

To cultivate an elegant walk there is no better exercise than walking round and round a room with a light book balanced on the head. To keep the book in position the head must be held erect, with the chin well drawn in and the shoulders well back. The eyes should look level; in fact, the advice of an American that one should "look every one in the face as if they owed you ten dollars" is excellent. For the eyes to look level the head must be held in the correct position, so that the advice certainly will help to ensure a good head carriage.

Exercises are also necessary to obtain a graceful walk and good carriage. The woman who is stiff in her movements will never be graceful. Further, stiffness always gives an impression of age.

An excellent exercise for securing a supple, graceful carriage is the following, which should be practised for a few minutes night and morning:

Stand behind a tall chair, placing the hands lightly on the back rail. Bend from the knees till almost squatting on the heels. Rise and repeat. The body should be kept rigid from the waist-line, with the shoulders well back and head up, eyes looking level.

At first the exercise should be taken slowly, but as the muscles grow accustomed to the movements the pace may be increased, and later the help of the chair can be dispensed with and the exercise taken with the hands placed lightly on the hips.

Any one who has watched Russian dancers will have noticed that they can squat on the heels and rise again with the greatest agility, and it is this exercise which gives the greatest suppleness to every muscle in the body.

Another exercise which will help, consists of standing against a door or wall and pressing the heels, shoulders, back of the head, and elbows against the door. Then, without moving the elbows, endeavour to touch the door with the back of the hands.

Touching the toes will also help. For this, stand erect, bend the body at the waist, and try to touch the toes with the tips of the fingers, keeping the knees rigid. Those who have neglected physical exercises for some time will find this rather difficult at first, but with practice there should be no difficulty except in the case of women who are very stout.

<u>Chamois Leather.</u> The woman whose complexion is inclined to be greasy and has an unbecoming shine should keep a piece of very soft chamois leather on her dressing-table. After cleansing the face the leather should be passed over the skin, and if it has previously been dipped in the powder bowl, the skin will look soft and smooth and the pores will not "give".

The leather will also be found very useful for smoothing the skin after applying liquid powder. Allow the powder to dry on the skin, then dust over with the chamois leather. This treatment is specially to be recommended for the arms, for powder on arms treated in this way does not rub off on the wearer's dress or on her dancing partner's coat sleeves.

mind an' put the chamois back after for the windas!

18

<u>Chaps</u>. Nothing is more uncomfortable or more disfiguring than rough, chapped hands, and the thinner and more sensitive the skin the more easily it chaps. During the colder months of the year the hands should always be thoroughly dried, and after drying dusted over with a little fine oatmeal. This has a very softening effect.

Keep a jar of the oatmeal handy and put a little in the palm of one hand, then "wash" the hands with it, rubbing it well into the backs and fingers. Dust off with a perfectly dry towel. If this is done every time the hands are washed and dried there will be no fear of chapping the skin, however frosty the weather.

When the skin has already become chapped rub in a mixture of glycerine and rosewater at night, after thoroughly cleansing the hands, and sleep in loose-fitting cotton gloves. The glycerine is rather a heroic remedy for it makes the chapped skin smart when first applied. It is, however, really effective and will cure the roughness after two or three applications.

<u>Cheeks, Hollow</u>. When the cheeks are too thin and hollow, giving a worn, drawn look to the face, try massaging them with a little oil of sweet almonds, mixed with pure lanolin, in the proportion of ½ an oz. of lanolin to 1½ oz. of the oil.

Melt lanolin and add oil. Beat together. Bathe the cheeks with warm water, dry, put a little of the cream in the centre of the cheek and massage it round and round, very gently pinching the flesh just below the line of the cheek bone, and using the pads of the thumb and first finger.

One should also practise bubble blowing. Blowing imaginary bubbles will help to fill out the cheeks.

Lanolin [Latin lana=wool + Latin oleum=oil] is wool wax, wool fat, wool grease, or anhydrous wool fat. It is the greasy yellow substance secreted by glands of wool-bearing animals, most of which comes from domestic sheep. It is similar to wax, and can be used as an ointment for the skin or as water-proofing agent. It is also used as an ingredient in the commercial manufacture of polishing products. It is lanolin's waterproofing properties which allow sheep to shed rainwater from their coats. Extraction of Lanolin is achieved by pressing the sheep's wool between rollers. When wool is processed for the textile use, the lanolin is removed.

Chilblains. Chilblains are always a sign that the circulation is poor and the "patient" is in need of a good tonic. Cod liver oil is excellent, but when this is objected to one should see what an iron tonic will do to tone up the general system.

To prevent chilblains keep the hands and feet warm, massage the hands well every time they are washed, and do not hold them near a fire after returning from a walk in the cold.

Once a chilblain has broken it should be treated by a doctor.

Chin. A double chin is one of the most ageing and unbecoming of all beauty blemishes. Occasionally this double chin is the result of an incorrect poise of the head, and those who stoop over books or work continually often develop a second chin without being too plump in any other way.

In such cases the trouble is due to sagging muscles, and exercises and massage, with a good astringent lotion, will reduce it. When the double chin is due to an accumulation of fatty tissue it is more difficult to treat, for as the fat is dissolved the skin must be restored to its former elasticity or a baggy condition with loose flabby skin beneath the chin will result.

To massage a double chin place the hands on either jaw bone with the thumbs meeting immediately beneath the chin, and with firm hard strokes work the flesh along beneath the jaw towards the ears. No cream should be used when massaging a double chin. Dust the hands with talcum powder and massage for at least ten minutes. Then douche beneath the chin with very cold water. This is to brace the muscles and strengthen them, and is excellent for treating a double chin resulting from a incorrect poise of the head.

To reduce the second chin when it is due to an accumulation of fatty tissue, dip the fingers in a reducing lotion and work it into the fat to break down the tissues. Place the thumb and first finger of both hands immediately beneath the chin and pinch and knead it, using the thumb and first finger of both hands, working towards the lobes of the ears.

Next, with firm, hard movements stroke from immediately beneath the chin towards the base of the throat, starting from the centre beneath the chin and working towards the sides. Keep up the massage for at least fifteen minutes and dab on some of the astringent lotion.

What about Daphne's third chin?

Chin-Strap. It is not always advisable to wear a chin-strap. The heat generated by the strap helps to weaken the muscles, and while it may dissolve some of the fatty tissue it tends to make the skin beneath the chin loose and flabby.

WHICH LITTLE UR-CHIN WROTE THIS?

Exercises for reducing a Double Chin.—1. Stand erect, head well up, shoulders drawn back, and abdomen tucked in. Take a deep breath, then clench the teeth and turn the head to the right, looking over the right shoulder as far as possible without moving the body. Return to original position and turn the head towards the left, looking over the left shoulder. Rest and repeat.

2. Stand erect, head well up, and shoulders back. Clench the teeth and drop the head on the chest. With a quick jerking movement toss the head upwards and backwards as far as possible, looking towards the ceiling. Rest and repeat. Both these exercises should be practised from ten to twenty times every night and morning, and when possible occasionally during the day.

Chiropody. The dainty woman gives as much attention to her feet as to her hands, and her toe nails are as carefully pedicured as her finger nails are manicured. Toe nails should always be cut straight across, for any other method encourages in-growing toe nails, a most painful condition.

Colds. There is no ailment that is more unromantic and which excites less sympathy than a cold. Yet it is one of the most trying and certainly the most beauty-destroying, of minor ills. It reddens the nose, makes the eyes dull and watery, and often brings sores to the lips.

The quickest and simplest way of curing a cold is to take two or three drops of oil of

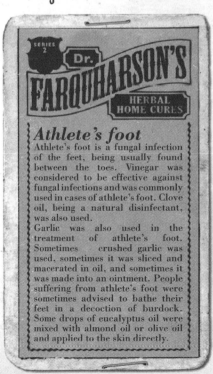

SERIES 2

Dr. FARQUHARSON'S

HERBAL HOME CURES

Athlete's foot

Athlete's foot is a fungal infection of the feet, being usually found between the toes. Vinegar was considered to be effective against fungal infections and was commonly used in cases of athlete's foot. Clove oil, being a natural disinfectant, was also used.

Garlic was also used in the treatment of athlete's foot. Sometimes crushed garlic was used, sometimes it was sliced and macerated in oil, and sometimes it was made into an ointment. People suffering from athlete's foot were sometimes advised to bathe their feet in a decoction of burdock. Some drops of eucalyptus oil were mixed with almond oil or olive oil and applied to the skin directly.

eucalyptus on a lump of sugar at the first sign of the trouble. Also put half a dozen drops of the oil in a basin of boiling water, tie a light bandage over the eyes, and throwing a towel over the head, inhale the steam for several minutes.

The towel should hang well down over the sides of the basin to keep the steam in, and the patient ought to go to bed immediately, and keep in the same temperature for 24 hours. At the end of that time all traces of the cold should have disappeared.

If the cold has been neglected it will take longer to cure, but even in the most advanced stages the methods referred to above will effect some relief.

When a sore, produced by a cold, has formed, a camphor–ice ball gently rubbed over it will help in curing it quickly and permanently.

<u>Combs.</u> When choosing a comb be careful to see that the teeth are quite blunt. Sharp teeth tend to irritate the scalp and encourage dandruff.

If the hair is greasy choose a comb with fine teeth, and when combing the hair, comb it in every direction, using first the large teeth and then the side of the comb with fine teeth. The more hair is combed the more wavy it will become. In the mornings it is a good plan to shake a comb out in luke–warm water before combing the hair. This helps to induce a wave, especially if the hair is pinched into waves directly the comb is removed.

Learn To Make and Play a Comb Kazoo.

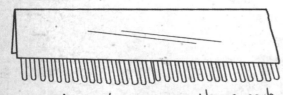

If you can hum a tune, you can play a comb.
Start a Comb Band in your street.
Get on Top o' The Pops.

Get ane o' Daphne's combs.
Fold a bit of paper over it.

To play – Press your lips against the comb.

Hum a tune and keep the comb still. As you hum, the vibration will cause the paper to rattle. The result is like a kazoo.

<u>To cure a Corn.</u> A homely, but very effective, remedy for a corn consists in binding a slice of raw tomato over the corn, renewing the tomato every night and morning till the corn becomes so loose that it can be easily removed.

Painting the corn with tincture of iodine is another simple remedy which is often all that is required to bring about a cure, but in obstinate cases it is best to obtain the services of a chiropodist and remove the trouble once and for all.

Those with a tendency to gout generally suffer more with hard corns than others, and when there is such a tendency precautions should be taken to wear only well-fitted shoes, and the feet ought to be dusted morning and night with the following powder: Oxide of zinc 2 drachms, boric acid 2 drachms, powdered starch 1 oz. Mix together and pass through a sieve, then place in a tin with a perforated lid.

When a corn is very painful, relief can generally be obtained by soaking a small piece of cotton-wool in turpentine and binding it over the corn. This seldom fails to give relief, and when the treatment is repeated daily will eventually effect a cure.

Soft corns are generally due to excessive perspiration, and the feet should be dusted with the powder given above and the insides of the stockings sprinkled with talcum powder before being slipped on. A piece of tissue paper, folded to fit over the corn, in several thicknesses, worn regularly, is often sufficient to cure the trouble. The paper should be changed two or three times during the day.

Callouses are merely larger forms of corn, but seldom contain the "core" found in the ordinary corn. Mostly they appear under the ball of the big toe, and occasionally

THESE mInTS TASTE AWFUL!

beneath that of the little toe. These are best treated by first soaking in warm water, scraping them, and painting with tincture of iodine. Any chemist will supply small pads, which can be worn to give relief when the pain or inconvenience is severe.

<u>Complexion.</u> The woman who would possess a clear, smooth skin with a pretty, natural colour must give it proper attention. Hard water and a too-strong soap is ruinous to the complexion, and soap should never be used with cold water.

To cleanse the face with cream is far better than to use soap and water, but those who feel that soap is necessary in their particular case should be careful to choose a super-fatted one. Apply it with luke-warm water, rinse all traces carefully off, then sponge the skin with cold water.

Whether you use soap and water or cream, never fail to cleanse the face thoroughly before sleep. This is specially necessary for those who use day-cream and powder, for to leave any form of "make-up" on the skin during sleep is to encourage blackheads and enlarged pores.

<u>Cleansing the Face.</u> Always keep a good supply of cotton-wool on your dressing-table. Take a piece and wipe the face and throat. Next dip the fingers in a good cleansing cream and spread it over both face and throat. With the tips of the fingers work the cream well into the pores, rubbing always in an upward and outward direction.

Take another piece of wool, or a clean, soft piece of butter-muslin, and wipe off all the cream. The face will feel fresh and clean, and the skin will be able to breathe during the hours of sleep, which is essential if it is to look fresh and clear next morning.

Remember that a good complexion is not made by external applications alone. Creams

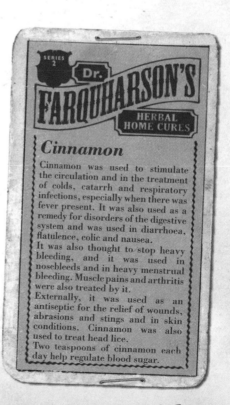

SERIES 2

Dr. FARQUHARSON'S HERBAL HOME CURES

Cinnamon

Cinnamon was used to stimulate the circulation and in the treatment of colds, catarrh and respiratory infections, especially when there was fever present. It was also used as a remedy for disorders of the digestive system and was used in diarrhoea, flatulence, colic and nausea.

It was also thought to stop heavy bleeding, and it was used in nosebleeds and in heavy menstrual bleeding. Muscle pains and arthritis were also treated by it.

Externally, it was used as an antiseptic for the relief of wounds, abrasions and stings and in skin conditions. Cinnamon was also used to treat head lice.

Two teaspoons of cinnamon each day help regulate blood sugar.

and lotions will help, but the clear beauty of the skin depends upon deep breathing and the drinking of sufficient water. Water renews the tissues and helps to clear the skin of pimples and blotches.

Sleep is another necessity to a clear, smooth skin. At least seven hours' sleep must be taken by the woman who would keep a smooth, unlined complexion. The bedroom should be dark but well ventilated, and the bedclothes light in weight though sufficiently warm.

When the Skin is Sallow. Cleanse it with oatmeal mixed to a paste with lukewarm water, and take every morning a teaspoonful of pure olive oil mixed with an equal quantity of grape juice.

The regular daily use of a good feeding cream is essential if the complexion is to be kept in perfect condition. The cream should be applied every night and allowed to soak into the pores before being wiped off. Allow it to soak in for about ten minutes, by which time the pores will have absorbed all that they are capable of absorbing. Wipe off, and if the skin is naturally greasy, apply a little mild astringent lotion on a pad of cotton-wool.

No chocolate creams Daphne!

Creams. Whether the skin is naturally dry or greasy, the regular use of a cream is essential if the skin is to be kept soft, smooth, and free from lines and wrinkles. The choice of the right cream must depend upon the type of skin to be treated. A very dry skin requires a cream with plenty of oils, which replaces the lack of natural oil in the skin, while a greasy skin requires one with rather less. But all types require a good feeding cream applied occasionally.

Feeding Cream. An excellent feeding cream can be made as follows: Take ½ oz. of white wax, ½ oz. of spermaceti, and 2 oz. of lanolin. Put the wax and spermaceti in an earthenware jar and stand the jar in a pan of hot water till both have melted. Add 4 oz. of pure oil of sweet almonds and stir together.

Remove the jar from the pan and add, while beating to a cream, ¼ oz. of extract of witch-hazel and a drachm of simple tincture of benzoin. The witch-hazel must be added a few drops at a time and the benzoin a drop at a time, and cream beaten till quite cold. Place in pomade pots and cover.

A Filling—out Cream for filling out the neck, arms, etc.: Take ½ oz. of cocoa butter, 1 oz. of pure lanolin, and ½ oz. of spermaceti. Put these in an earthenware jar and melt on the stove or in a pan of hot water. Stir together and add, stirring all the time, 3 oz. of pure olive oil. When mixed, remove the jar from the heat and beat to a cream, adding 60 drops of simple tincture of benzoin while beating.

Before applying this cream the skin should be bathed with hot water and dried, so that pores may be relaxed and ready to absorb it. It will be found excellent for filling out the too—thin arms, neck, shoulders, or bust.

A Cream for the Hands. A cream for whitening and softening neglected hands may be made by beating together 1 oz. of zinc ointment, 1 oz. of pure lanolin, and ½ oz. of olive oil. Melt the lanolin and zinc ointment together, add the oil, and beat together. This is excellent for hands that are dry and wrinkled.

Cream of Cucumbers. Take three cucumbers, wipe them over with a damp cloth, and cut into slices about half an inch thick. Place in a jar and pour over them 6 oz. of oil of sweet almonds. Stand the jar in a pan of hot water on the side of the stove and allow to simmer for five or six hours. Strain through muslin and measure.

Now, to each 6 oz. of the liquid add 2 oz. of lanolin and 1 oz. of white wax. Warm it up till the wax and lanolin melt, and then stir thoroughly. Beat to a cream, and while beating add ½ drachm of simple tincture of benzoin and a few drops of essence of rose or violets to scent the cream. Place in pomade pots and cover.

During very cold weather all massage creams should be slightly warmed before being used.

<u>Cleansing Cream.</u> To make a simple, inexpensive cleansing cream, place ¼ lb. of the best lard in a basin. Pour over it sufficient boiling water to fill the basin. Leave till the water becomes quite cold and the lard floats on the top. Pour off the water and repeat the process twice more. Then put the lard in a clean basin, add 2 tablespoonfuls of rosewater, and beat to a cream.

"Crows-feet" is the name by which the fine little lines which form at the corners of the eyes are generally known. These lines may be due to eye-strain or the passing of the years. Occasionally they are due to the habit of screwing up the eyes when laughing. But whatever the cause they add several years to a woman's apparent age and should be treated as soon as they appear.

Ha! Ha!
CROWS-FEET

The skin around the eyes is the most delicate and the most easily stretched, and when treating "crows-feet" the cream or oil used should be lightly tapped into the skin. Never rub around the eyes, for rubbing stretches the skin and deepens and increases the wrinkles and lines already formed.

When the skin is thin and sensitive the use of oil will be found better than cream. First bathe the closed eyes with warm water, dry by dabbing with a soft cloth; and, with the tip of the second finger, spread a thin layer of oil (or cream, if the latter is preferred) over the skin. Then, using the first, second, and third finger, tap it into the pores, tapping lightly as if playing the piano. The eyes should look upwards while the tapping is given, and when all the oil has been absorbed the closed eyes should be sponged with cold water.

When cream is chosen, a good feeding one is the most satisfactory; when oil is preferred, it is best to use oil of sweet almonds.

Those who have lines and wrinkles round the eyes should remember that to waken in bright light is very injurious and invariably encourages lines and wrinkles round the eyes. Let the bedroom be well ventilated, but dark, or, if it is not possible to have the windows properly screened, arrange the bed so that the head will not face the window.

When the crows-feet are due to eye-strain or tired eyes, benefit can be obtained by resting in a darkened room with pads of cotton-wool squeezed out in cold weak tea or luke-warm boric lotion on the lids.

Herbs at Home

Lily of the Valley

Lily of the valley is also known as May blossom and wood lily.

Its main use was as a heart stimulant, like the foxglove, but it was also used to treat sinusitis and dizziness in cases of fluid retention. Externally it was used for rheumatic pain.

Burnett's Herbal Teas
"Nature's Wonders"

Dentifrice. Whether one prefers a paste or liquid for cleansing the teeth must depend upon individual taste, but the ideal is to use a paste at night and a liquid in the morning.

A few drops of peroxide of hydrogen added to the water used is always beneficial. Peroxide of hydrogen is an antiseptic and also helps to whiten the teeth. It is even more necessary to use this when there are any false teeth fixed on a bar or bridge, when there are any "dead" teeth (teeth of which the nerve has been killed), or much cigarette smoking is indulged in.

Deodorants. A home-made deodorant is seldom satisfactory. It is best to get one of the many excellent preparations on the market, but those who are troubled with perspiring feet will find sponging with equal portions of vinegar and water a great help.

A deodorant powder can be made by mixing 20 grains of salicylic acid, 2 drachms of powdered starch and ½ an oz. of powdered alum. This should be dusted on the skin after it has been sponged with warm water and dried.

<u>Depilatories.</u> Depilatories for the removal of superfluous hair are only a temporary remedy. Electrolysis is the one permanent cure, and this must be carried out by a really reliable operator or the roots may be left behind or perhaps, even worse, little pinholes made.

Besides the use of a depilatory and electrolysis, there are two other ways of removing a growth. The hairs may be pulled out singly with a pair of toilet tweezers and a drop of eau-de-Cologne applied to each spot from which a hair has been removed. When the root is removed with the hair, this is one of the best methods, for the hair will not grow again on that particular spot, and if a weak solution of peroxide is used regularly after removing the hairs there is every reason to hope that others will not appear.

The other method consists of bleaching the hairs with a mixture of peroxide of hydrogen (10 vol.), and liquid ammonia, 1 teaspoonful of the peroxide to 3 (not more) drops of cloudy ammonia. This should be painted over each individual hair with a fine camel's-hair brush and the liquid allowed to dry on the hair. For under-arm toilet the best and simplest method is shaving with a safety razor. A mixture of peroxide and rosewater, 2 parts of peroxide (10 vol.) to 1 part rosewater should be dabbed over the skin after the shave. Shaving with the safety razor is also the best method for any growth of hair on the arms and legs followed with sponging with the peroxide and rosewater mixture.

<u>Diet.</u> The woman who would have a clear fresh complexion, and a slender figure must remember that diet is of the greatest importance. Nothing whatever should be taken between meals, and those who would lose weight should make the chief meal of the day the midday one.

Brown bread is better than white, both for the complexion and figure, and wholemeal is the best. Butter is not fattening, and is essential for the nervous woman. In fact, butter is a nerve food and should not be omitted from the daily menu even when a reducing diet is taken. Those who wish to put on weight should take plenty of milk, milky puddings, and all forms of cereals, fatty meats, bacon, and eggs. Fish should be included— mackerel and herrings, kippers, salmon, and skate. Vegetables, which grow under the ground, such as potatoes and turnips, are good for the too thin. Several small meals are to be preferred to three heavy ones, and the rule for those who would put on weight is to eat little and often. A glass of milk taken warm and slowly sipped at bedtime will help, and tea should be made with boiling milk instead of boiling water.

The stout woman ought to avoid all those foods mentioned above and take tomatoes, pineapple, and grapefruit. A glass of hot water, to which the juice of a lemon has been added, taken the first thing in the morning, in place of early tea, will help, and at least a pint of hot water should be sipped before going to bed.

<u>Milk and Potato Diet.</u> This diet was at one time considered excellent for reducing, and for those whom it suits it certainly is. It consists of taking nothing but milk and potatoes on two days a week. The allowance is 1 lb. of boiled potatoes and 1 quart of milk for the whole day.

The first ½ pint of milk is taken at the usual breakfast hour. The second at eleven in the morning. The third is taken at lunch with 1 lb. potatoes boiled and eaten without butter. The last ½ pint is taken at six in the evening. Nothing whatever may be taken on the milk and potato days except what has been mentioned. On other days the usual foods are permitted, omitting all those regarded as flesh forming.

There is no doubt whatever that the most fattening meal is the one taken in the evening, and it is becoming more and more the rule with women who are keen on reducing to have only a light meal of eggs, cheese, or fruit at night.

All spirits, sweet wines, cocktails, and beers or stout must be avoided by those eager to lose weight. Lemon and water, or lemon squash may be taken, but the best of all drinks for them is plain water.

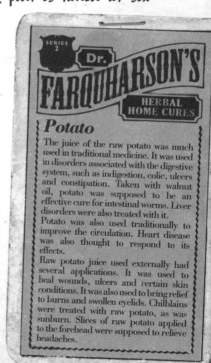

SERIES 2

Dr.

FARQUHARSON'S

HERBAL HOME CURES

Potato

The juice of the raw potato was much used in traditional medicine. It was used in disorders associated with the digestive system, such as indigestion, colic, ulcers and constipation. Taken with walnut oil, potato was supposed to be an effective cure for intestinal worms. Liver disorders were also treated with it. Potato was also used traditionally to improve the circulation. Heart disease was also thought to respond to its effects. Raw potato juice used externally had several applications. It was used to heal wounds, ulcers and certain skin conditions. It was also used to bring relief to burns and swollen eyelids. Chilblains were treated with raw potato, as was sunburn. Slices of raw potato applied to the forehead were supposed to relieve headaches.

DAPHnE IS On A SEAFOOD DIET SHE SEES FOOD AnD EATS IT !

The latest slimming diet from Hollywood consists of hard–boiled eggs and tomatoes. For this three days are set apart on which the chief meal of the day consists of two hard–boiled eggs and two tomatoes. This is the midday meal. The tomatoes and eggs are eaten without condiments of any kind, with a little rye bread and butter. For breakfast on those days, tea and a slice of thin toast is all that is allowed, and for the evening meal only fruit such as grapefruit, apples, or a couple of tomatoes. No afternoon tea is allowed. This diet has been found very successful, and has the advantage that on other days anything that is fancied may be taken.

Ears. Small, prettily–shaped ears are always attractive provided they do not stand out too far from the head. Under artificial light a touch of rouge to the lobes of the ears increases the brightness of the eyes, especially when they are very dark.

When too large the ears can be made to appear smaller if the cartilage at the extreme edge is lightly rouged.

Ears which are Too Prominent. Prominent ears, which stand out from the head, are generally due to carelessness on the part of mother or nurse during infancy.

When placing a child in his cot, care should be taken to see that the ears are pressed flat against the head, for once adult age has been reached very little can be done to remedy the disfigurement. A cap can be made, and worn at night, consisting of a piece of elastic arranged to fit round the head, or a shingle cap can be worn instead, with a small piece of elastic sewn over the ear flaps.

The ears should be bathed with warm water, dried gently, and pressed firmly back before the cap is put on. Up to the age of 16 wearing such a cap every night will help in correcting too–prominent ears, but after that age very little can be done, and it is better to try and arrange the hair to hide the defect.

HORACE HAS
AWFY BIG EARS !

Ear-Rings. Whether your choice is for a "stud," a long ear-ring, or the gipsy shape, must depend upon your type of feature and very largely upon your neck. The woman with a long, slender neck can wear long hanging ear-rings, and if her colouring is striking and she can "carry off" unusual ornaments, her ear-rings may be as long and barbaric looking as she wishes.

If she is petite and has a short plump neck she should choose a stud ear-ring, and only those with dark hair and vivid colouring should wear a gipsy ear-ring. Ear-rings brighten the eyes, except diamond ear-rings which tend to make them appear hard, and although they always tend to add a few years to a woman's apparent age, are decidedly smart on those whom they suit.

It is not necessary to have the ears pierced to wear ear-rings. Almost every style can be obtained with screw fastenings, and even if those of your choice have wires, any jeweller will remove the wires and affix screws for a couple of shillings.

Eczema. Although, strictly speaking, eczema is not exactly a beauty subject often there is a slight touch of it on the face, especially during the early spring, which can be treated without the aid of a doctor.

Eczema in such a case appears as a roughness of the skin generally around the mouth and chin or on the forehead. A little zinc ointment, rubbed gently into the "patches", will effect a cure if persevered with for a few days. No soap should be used to the face while there is any trace of the

Health & Beauty Monthly

Eczema

ECZEMA is a condition of the skin in which the skin becomes red and itchy and starts to flake and weep.

A tea made from marigold flowers was an old cure for eczema. Another internal cure was a drink made from hot water, lemon juice, honey and cayenne pepper, while yet another was a decoction of dock.

A cure applied externally involved boiling a handful of watercress in water, straining the mixture, allowing it to cool and then bathing the areas affected with eczema two or three times a day. Watercress was also taken internally to try and effect a cure.

A broth made from carrot was applied to affected areas to relieve itching from eczema. Olive oil was used to soothe skin affected by the condition, as was glycerine. Bathing with a little vinegar and water was also thought to soothe skin irritation.

Cucumber juice was also advocated as a soother of inflamed skin, and burdock poultices were sometimes applied to help heal the skin. Marigold used externally was also thought to help the healing process and reduce inflammation. Lemon balm was also applied externally to reduce inflammation.

A poultice was made from the leaves and flowers of borage to relieve eczema, while the root and bark of elder was made into an ointment to cure it.

trouble, and plenty of green vegetables and fruit included in the daily diet.

Occasionally indulging in rather more sugar than is usual will bring up a patch of eczema, and if the roughness does not yield to the simple treatment suggested above, a doctor should be consulted.

Eggs.—As Diet. Eggs are an excellent article of diet for the too thin. Those who would lose weight should not take them fried. Lightly boiled or poached or as hard-boiled eggs, but not fried or in the form of omelettes.

Egg Mask, the. This is excellent for removing fine lines round the eyes. To make it, break an egg and separate the white from the yolk. Put the white in a little basin and beat it stiffly, as for a meringue, adding, while beating, half a teaspoon of lemon juice or five drops of eau-de-Cologne.

Sponge the skin with hot water, dry by dabbing with a soft towel, and, with the tip of the finger, smear the egg mixture over the lines, allowing it to dry on. Leave for the night and wash off next morning with soft lukewarm water.

The white of an egg, lightly spread over "crows-feet" or lines around the eyes, will "fade" them for a few hours, and is excellent for use on special occasions. The effect however is not permanent.

Egg Shampoo. An egg shampoo is very beneficial for hair that is turning prematurely

EGG

Eggs have long been regarded as being exceptionally nutritious. Nowadays we tend to eat fewer of them because they are high in cholesterol. In folk remedies, however, they were much valued as an easily digested food for invalids and convalescents to build up their strength.

Raw eggs or very lightly boiled eggs were used as a tonic. Stomach disorders were also treated with eggs in this way, eggs being thought to be helpful in cases of indigestion, constipation and diarrhoea.

Various light foods based on eggs, such as egg custard, were given to invalids. Drinks based on eggs were also given to invalids to give them more strength. These included eggnog, one recipe for which involved beating a egg yolk with milk and then adding some brandy and a beaten egg white. A small amount of lime water was thought to make this more digestible.

Egg white, beaten up in milk, was taken as an antidote to some corrosive poisons.

Eggs were also used externally to soothe the skin. The white of eggs was applied in layers, time being given for each layer to dry, to cracked nipples in nursing mothers, to babies' bottoms affected by nappy rash and to the skin of people affected by sunburn.

One cure for burns involved eggs. The whites of eggs were beaten until stiff and spread over the burn.

Another use for eggs was to prevent hair from falling out. In this remedy eggs were beaten, mixed with water and rubbed into the scalp. This was left on overnight and washed out the next morning.

Eggs were also used to shampoo the hair to improve its general condition.

grey or for reddish—brown hair, for the sulphur in the egg yolk helps to arrest the greyness and brings out the brighter tints in reddish—brown hair.

To make the shampoo, beat up one or more eggs, as required, with one tablespoonful of lukewarm water for each egg, and a teaspoonful of fine shredded soap. Beat to a foamy mass, adding, while beating, a tablespoonful of bay rum. Wet the scalp and hair with lukewarm water, and shampoo the egg mixture well into the roots and through the hair.

Rinse off in three separate waters, adding to the last rinsing water a tablespoonful of white wine vinegar.

Elbows. To improve sharp—pointed elbows massage with cream at night and in the morning rub in a little fine oatmeal, mixed to a paste with lukewarm water. Take a lump of the cream, place it in the palm of one hand, holding the hand to the elbow of the other arm and curving it like a cup, rub round and round till all the cream has been absorbed. Leave a little on the skin and wrap a piece of butter muslin round the elbow to keep the grease on the skin. In the morning bathe with warm water and rub in a small amount of sweet almonds, sponging it off before dressing.

Red Elbows. When the elbows, besides being pointed are red, get a lemon, cut it in half and remove the pips. Place the elbow into one—half of the lemon, pressing it firmly in, and rub round and round. Let the lemon juice soak into the skin and rinse off with lukewarm water.

If you would keep your elbows rounded and white do not sit with them on the table. Nothing makes them more unattractive. Pressing them on the table makes them pointed and red, while constantly keeping the arms bent in that position spoils the shape of the upper arm.

Elderly Spread, the. Spreading of the hips, commonly called the "elderly spread", is generally the result of lack of sufficient exercise.

Walking will help to prevent it and exercise will be found of great help.

A good corset should be worn by the woman who finds that her figure is spreading, and it should reach well down over the hips.

<u>Exercise.</u> Daily exercise is essential for both health and beauty. At least half an hour's walk should be taken every day whatever the weather. Walking in the rain will not do any harm; in fact it is beneficial to the complexion, provided one is suitably clad. Given good foot gear, and a mackintosh, a walk in the rain can be very enjoyable. The only precaution necessary is to change into dry things on returning home.

But to be beneficial a walk, must be brisk. Sauntering along, looking into shop windows, is of no use. It does not bring the muscles into play nor increase the circulation of the blood both of which are essential to a really beneficial walk.

Early morning is the best time for a beauty walk and those who can manage to walk part of the way to their business will find it helpful for both health and beauty. The complexion will be clearer, the eyes bright and there will be a sense of general well-being that was not experienced before.

<u>Exercises for Reducing Weight.</u> Exercises for reducing weight must be carried out regularly and it is best to fix one particular time and practise them at that hour each day. To practise one day and neglect to do so the next is quite useless, the benefit gained is lost in the interval.

By exercising the muscles regularly they regain their lost elasticity and the figure loses the heavy aged appearance which stiff muscles and superfluous flesh always gives to a woman.

<u>For Reducing the Waist Line.</u> I. Stand erect, with the shoulders well back, and the chin up, eyes level. Raise the arms, with the fingers stretched out straight above the head, keeping the elbows rigid. Bend at the waist towards the left and touch the floor with the fingers of the left hand.

Return to original position and bend towards the right, touching the floor with the fingers of the right hand. Rest and repeat. This exercise should be taken slowly at first, but the speed increased as the muscles at the waist grow accustomed to it.

2. Sit on the floor and stretch the legs out in front, keeping the knees rigid. Bend at the waist and stretch forwards, touching the toes with the fingers. Return to original position and lower the body backwards as far as possible without actually lying on the back. Rise and bend forwards touching the toes again.

This exercise will be found rather difficult at first but with practice it should become easy and it is one of the best for making the waist slim and supple.

To reduce the Hips. 1. For this there is nothing better than rolling on the floor. Lie flat on the floor, with the face downwards, throw the arms above the head and roll over and over round the room. Roll as quickly as possible, for the quicker the roll the better the results.

2. Lie on the floor, face downwards, bend the legs at the knees, and passing the arms behind the back, clasp the ankles with the hands. In this position rock backwards and forwards while resting on the abdomen. The head should be held well up while practising.

3. Crawling is also very beneficial in reducing a too-large hip measurement. For this stretch out flat on the floor. Gradually raise the body till it rests on the hands and toes and lower the head till the body represents an inclined plane.

In this position crawl round and round the room several times, propelling the body slowly by the hands and toes.

To reduce the Legs. 1. Sit on a high stool, with the legs hanging loosely on either side and the feet about 10 in. from the ground. Take a light cane and hold it with both hands in front on a level with the waist.

Now work the feet as though propelling a bicycle. Practise this for from ten to twenty minutes, but do not overtire the muscles at first.

2. Stand erect, with the arms hanging at the sides, shoulder back and

chin up. Raise the right foot, with the knee bent, till the knee is on a level with the hip. Count five and lower repeating the exercise first with one foot then with the other. Practise for from ten to fifteen times with each foot.

To reduce the Abdomen. 1. Kneel on the floor, keeping the shoulders well back and the abdomen tucked in. Raise the arms above the head, keeping them close to the shoulders and stretching upwards in an endeavour to reach some high point. Rest and repeat from ten to twenty times.

2. Stand erect, shoulders back and abdomen tucked in. Bend forwards at the waist and touch the toes. Rise, throwing the arms upwards and outwards as far as they will go. Lower the body again, bending at the waist, and repeat. Practise this from twenty to thirty times daily.

All exercises whether for reducing or increasing weight should be practised before an open window, and only very light clothing should be worn. A bathing suit or gymnasium costume is the ideal. An exercise should be discontinued as soon as any feeling of fatigue is experienced.

It is best to start with two or three practices a couple of times and increase the number gradually than to overtire the muscles at first.

Expression. A bright, cheery expression should be cultivated. If the corners of the mouth are allowed to droop the expression is one of depression and a sulky look is given to the whole face. Keep the corners of the mouth turned up and a smiling effect is obtained without any trouble.

Bright eyes and a happy smile make even a woman with plain features attractive, and both can be acquired with very little trouble.

Eyes.—The Care of the Eyes. Beautiful eyes can make even a plain face attractive, but those who do not possess large expressive eyes can make them clear and bright by giving them proper care.

Never work or read in a strong glare or too poor a light; either are equally bad for the sight. When reading or working let the light fall on the book or work from over the shoulder, and, if electric light is used, see the bulbs are properly shaded, for the light being strong is very trying to the eyes.

The Daily Eye-Bath. The eyes should be given an eye-bath every morning and always after being exposed to fog, dust, or a long motor journey. An eye-bath can be obtained from any chemist for sixpence, or one shilling, and an eye-lotion can be made at home from boric acid powder and rosewater.

The bath should be warm, and fresh lotion used for each eye. This is to prevent a cold, should there be one, or any other trouble, in one eye being conveyed to the other.

Eye-Lotion. To make the eye-lotion put a level teaspoonful of boric acid powder in a clean 8-oz. bottle. Add sufficient hot (not boiling) water to half-fill the bottle and shake till the powder has dissolved. Fill up the bottle with distilled rosewater and cork.

When required, half fill the eye-bath with the lotion and add sufficient hot water to make the whole lukewarm. Fit the "bath" to the eye and open and shut several times.

Should there be any feeling of discomfort on the lids bathe the closed eyes with a little of the lotion, using a pad of cotton-wool.

For Tired Eyes. If the eyes feel dull and tired take two pieces of cotton-wool, each large enough to fit over one eye, squeeze them out in boric acid lotion, and place one over each closed eye.

Wring a pocket handkerchief out in lukewarm water, fold it like a bandage and sprinkle 2 or 3 drops of eau-de-Cologne on it, lay it lightly across the eyes, and rest in a darkened room for about ten minutes.

This will refresh and help to brighten the eyes, and is an excellent treatment for improving the eyes before going to a dance or other entertainment.

Hollows beneath Eyes. The skin round the eyes should never be rubbed, for being the finest and most delicate on the face it is very easily stretched. To fill out the hollows spread some good feeding cream on the skin and allow it to soak into the pores.

Do this at night, leaving the cream thickly spread on till next morning, wipe it off very gently and sponge the closed eyes with cold water. Should the hollows be due to impaired health take an iron tonic and get all the sleep and fresh air possible.

Puffiness beneath Eyes. Puffiness beneath the eyes may be due to eyestrain, lack of sufficient sleep, or a slight kidney trouble. If the former, have the eyes tested for suitable glasses. Should lack of sufficient sleep be the cause the remedy is easy, while if kidney trouble is suspected the advice of the doctor should be sought. A little attention at the beginning will soon put matters right and prevent complications later.

For external treatment the skin beneath the eyes may be painted with a mixture of tannic acid and glycerine. Dissolve 20 grains of tannic acid in 1 oz. of glycerine and with a fine camel's-hair brush paint the mixture over the puffiness. Allow to remain on for several hours and wash off by dabbing the skin with a piece of cotton-wool dipped in lukewarm water.

The Whites of the Eyes. The whites of the eyes should be a clear bluish-white, and any sign of redness shows a strain on the sight or a slight cold in the eye, while a yellowish tinge is sign of "liver".

To remove the yellow tinge take a glass of hot water, to which the juice of a lemon has been added, every morning instead of early tea. No sugar may be added to the lemon and water.

Eye.—Exercises for the Eye. To keep the eyes in good condition they should be exercised as well as bathed.

Stand erect, with the head up and the eyes level. Look to the right as far as possible without turning the head, next to the left; to the right again, and to the left. Repeat from ten to twenty times.

Look upwards, then glance downwards as quickly as possible; upward and downwards several times.

These exercises are best practised after the daily eye-bath.

Eyebrows, the Care of. The eyebrows should be brushed every night and morning, and always after powdering the face, for complexion powder allowed to remain in the eyebrows helps to develop dandruff amongst the roots and will eventually spoil them.

A few drops of oil on the brush will give them a gloss and help to train them in the desired line. Two small brushes should be kept; one for applying the oil and the other dry.

First brush the brows from the eyes upwards then brush across the line.

Too-Light Eyebrows. When the eyebrows are too light they may be darkened naturally by the regular application of yellow vaseline rubbed into them every night, or by the use of an eyebrow pencil or eyebrow cosmetic in black or brown.

The colour should be chosen to tone with the hair and complexion.

To Pluck Eyebrows. When the eyebrows are too thick for beauty they can be plucked to a more delicate line, but once the plucking is started it must be continued, for the more the brows are plucked the more bushy they grow.

Unless they are extremely heavy and have been allowed to become much too thick it is best not to start plucking.

Eyelashes, the. Long, dark, curved eyelashes are an added beauty to the eyes, and if Nature has been niggardly in this respect a little care and attention will soon improve matters.

To Increase Growth. To make the eyelashes grow longer and thicker a little Golden Ointment should be used every night. Any chemist will supply the ointment and it should be applied with a fine camel's-hair brush to the extreme edges of the lids, along the roots of the lashes. Dip the point of the brush in the ointment and paint it over the roots.

To give the lashes a pretty curve tweak them upwards, using the thumb and first finger, or invest in one of the little gadgets sold for curling the lashes. These were first used in America, but can now be obtained at almost all the large stores.

Eyelids, the Care of the. Smooth, white, unwrinkled eyelids are essential to beautiful eyes and the lids should be bathed every morning with cold water and at night a drop of oil of sweet almonds very lightly massaged into them.

Close the eye and with the tip of the second finger, moistened with the oil, stroke the eyelid from the corner near the nose towards the outer corner. Treat first one eye then the other, and with a piece of cotton-wool wipe off any oil which may not have been absorbed.

The oil should not be allowed to enter the eye, for although it would not harm the sight it is uncomfortable.

Eyeshadows. Originally eyeshadows were only used for theatrical "make up", but now they are put up in such delicate colouring and so artistically treated that they can be used at any time and are employed by almost every woman for artificial light.

They may be obtained in either cream or compact form, and in shades of blue,

ALTERNATIVE EYE SHADOW METHOD — CAllIN' TAm mCSHUGGIE A BIG JESSIE!

43

mauve, green, brown, and grey. When choosing an eyeshadow select one that will harmonise with the colour of the eyes, a lighter shade being used for daylight than for the evening.

When there are many fine wrinkles around the eyes a touch of mauve eyeshadow applied lightly beneath them will almost entirely disguise the slight disfigurement.

Face.—To Cleanse. When the skin is fine and delicate, cream is a better agent for cleansing the face than soap and water. Cream penetrates to the pores and successfully rids them of any dirt or grime which a soot-laden town atmosphere invariably contains.

For a coarse greasy complexion an oatmeal paste is the best method of cleansing. This acts as a mild form of astringent and closes the pores of the skin. It also whitens and softens it. Those who prefer to use soap should be careful to choose a superfatted one and use it with lukewarm water. Soap should never be used to the skin of the face with cold water.

A dash of cold water to the face after whatever cleansing is used— soap, cream, or oatmeal—helps to make the skin fine and prevents blackheads and enlarged pores, provided it is very cold. Warm water relaxes the pores, cold closes them.

Face Packs. Face packs or "masks" are an extremely popular form of beauty treatment. They are given for clearing a muddy skin, for removing wrinkles, for toning up sagging muscles, and for bleaching purposes.

Another Egg Pack. To make an egg pack take the yolks of 2 perfectly fresh eggs and beat them up with 20 drops of simple tincture of benzoin to a stiff froth. The benzoin must be added a drop at a time while beating the eggs. Paint the mixture over the face and throat very thickly and allow it to dry on the skin. This will take about twenty minutes, or longer, and it must be perfectly dry before it is removed. It draws the impurities out of the skin, leaving it very clear and soft.

<u>Fuller's-Earth Pack.</u> Get a packet of Fuller's-earth and mix it to the paste with lukewarm water, adding 15 drops of simple tincture of benzoin and half a teaspoonful each of extract of witch-hazel and spirits of camphor. Should the paste be too thin add more Fuller's-earth to make it the right consistency to spread smoothly over the skin.

Apply it with a brush to the face and throat, leave to dry, and after it has dried allow it to remain on the face for twenty minutes.

To remove the egg or Fuller's-earth pack, wet a towel in lukewarm water and lay it over the face and wipe the pack off very gently, drawing the mixture upwards.

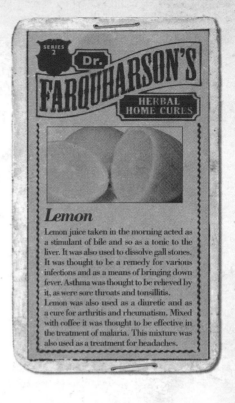

Lemon

Lemon juice taken in the morning acted as a stimulant of bile and so as a tonic to the liver. It was also used to dissolve gall stones. It was thought to be a remedy for various infections and as a means of bringing down fever. Asthma was thought to be relieved by it, as were sore throats and tonsillitis. Lemon was also used as a diuretic and as a cure for arthritis and rheumatism. Mixed with coffee it was thought to be effective in the treatment of malaria. This mixture was also used as a treatment for headaches.

<u>The Oil Pack.</u> For this take oil of sweet almonds. Half an ounce should be sufficient for one mask, and stir into it 10 drops of simple tincture of benzoin. With a soft brush paint the oil mixture over the entire face and throat.

Cut a piece of lint to cover the face and cut from it two holes for the eyes. Lay the lint over the oiled face and press very gently down on the skin. Leave for fifteen to twenty minutes. With a piece of cotton-wool wipe the oil from the face and dab on a little astringent lotion.

This is excellent for removing wrinkles. Before applying this mixture it should be placed in a bowl of hot water to warm the oil.

<u>The Grape-Juice Pack.</u> This is specially recommended for whitening the skin. Mash some grapes, preferably white grapes, and pass them through a sieve. Cleanse the face with warm water and spread the grape pulp over it. Cover with soft muslin mask as in the case of the oil, using muslin instead of lint, and leave for twenty minutes.

Wipe off and sponge the skin with cold water.

A Pack for a too-Thin Face. Cleanse the face thoroughly and sponge it over with warm water. Dry by patting gently with a soft towel. Cut a piece of butter-muslin in a round to cover the face, cutting out two holes for the eyes. Soak this in fresh dairy cream and place over the face, pressing it firmly on the skin. Leave for twenty minutes or longer.

General Hints on Face Packs. The skin must be thoroughly cleansed before the pack is applied. It should be left on the skin for 20 minutes or longer. The mask must be removed by dabbing the skin with a towel squeezed out in warm water.

Facial Massage. To preserve the contour of the face, remove lines and wrinkles, and improve the texture of the skin, there is no better treatment than massage.

The massage may be given either by hand or by electric means, and a good feeding cream should be used to lubricate the fingers when hand massage is given.

All massage should be given with an upward and outward movement, that is, from the jaws towards the cheek-bones and from the corners of the mouth towards the ears. When massaging the forehead, stroke from the eyebrows to the roots of the hair.

When the face is too full and the massage is intended to reduce it, the strokes should be firm and hard and very little cream applied. When it is to fill out the face or remove lines and wrinkles, the movements must be gentle and the skin lightly pinched and kneaded, a plentiful supply of cream being worked into the pores. After the massage any cream which has not been absorbed should be wiped off with a pad of cotton-wool and an astringent lotion dabbed over the face and throat.

Special Massage Movements. Massage to be beneficial in smoothing out lines and wrinkles and stimulating the muscles of the face must be gentle. Hard movements which result in dragging and stretching the skin only

47

make the lines they are intended to remove more pronounced.

Do not work backwards and forwards, always massage in the same direction over each part of the face; that is to say, when massaging from the corners of the mouth towards the ears do not work back from the ears to the corners of the mouth. When the lobes of the ears have been reached lift the fingers from the face and start at the corners of the mouth once more. Let the movements for the lines from nose to mouth be a circular crawling movement, quite gently, using the balls of the fingers only.

For Wrinkles on the Forehead. Starting at the outer side of the eyebrows gently stroke the forehead from that point to the roots of the hair; work in a slightly slanting line from the eyebrows over the temples to the roots of the hair.

For Frowning Wrinkles. For frowning wrinkles place the second finger of both hands on the space between the eyebrows, and stroke firmly towards the roots of the hair. The fingers should be close together at the start and the space between them increased as they near the roots of the hair.

To Restore the Youthful Line around the Chin and Jaws. Place the fingers of both hands immediately beneath the chin and pinch and knead the flesh along the line of the jaw from the centre, where the start is made, to beneath the ears. Continue with the pinching and kneading till the whole space beneath the chin has been treated.

When the Cheeks Sag and the Face Droops. For this the massage must be directed towards raising the muscles above the cheek-bone, and the massage should be given with light pinching movements

Health & Beauty Monthly

ESSENTIAL OILS

Oil Of Sweet Almonds

Sweet almond oil is a commonly used vegetable oil that is a carrier oil in aromatherapy massage because it has a very fine texture, and is quite easily absorbed into the skin, which it leaves soft and silky smooth, without being greasy. It is of the Rosaceae family and is related to the Peach and the Apricot. The Almond tree itself is a native to Barbary and is cultivated in the Mediterranean and the west coast of America. It has soft cream, yellow-centred blossom.
The oil is obtained from drying the kernels of the almond tree and it is softening and soothing and will help the skin to regain balance.

Eh, you've nae chance! Get a facelift! Paw

from just above the corners of the eyes to the roots of the hair below the temple.

The muscles situated here are of great importance, for upon them depends the youthful contour of the face. When they are flabby and have lost all elasticity the face drops and looks lined, tired, and old.

It is a good plan to start the facial massage here, and after the rest of the face has been treated to devote another few minutes to the same muscles.

Feet, the Care of the To make the feet graceful and supple walk about barefoot in your own room for a few minutes every day. Bathe the feet daily, and after drying massage the soles, instep, and ankles, dusting the fingers with a little talcum powder.

Hot, Perspiring Feet. Those who have much walking or standing to do often suffer with hot, perspiring feet. In such cases the feet should be bathed twice daily in hot water to which a handful of common salt has been added, dried, and massaged with a few drops of extract of witch-hazel. Talcum powder should be dusted over the insides of the stockings and on the soles of the shoes.

Flat Foot. There is no actual cure for flat-foot. Once the instep arch

Homemade Facial Treatments:

For deep cleansing of the skin, these can be considered as three kinds :

Cleansers are for an intensive, deep cleansing treatment. These masks have a clay or earth base. Clay has extraordinary drawing properties which extract impurities from the pores of the skin and will absorb excess sebum from the skin. Particularly used to get rid of stubborn blackheads. Allow time for these masks to become completely dry on your skin and rinse carefully with warm water.

Creams are used to refine and smooth the texture of the skin and will help dispel blemishes.

Gels are ideal for dry skin, these work with a base ingredient of fruits, herbs, minerals or vegetables. They dry to form a coating which can be easily removed, leaving the skin soft.

Original Oatmeal Mask Recipe:

Ingredients: 1 tablespoon of oatmeal
                     1egg yolk
                     Milk

Blend the oatmeal with milk - enough to make a paste. Beat in the egg yolk and fold it into the oatmeal paste. Pat on to the skin and leave for twenty minutes or so then rinse with lukewarm water.

The egg yolk helps to soften the skin and the coarse nature of the oatmeal helps to clean and nourish the skin.

Oatmeal & Cucumber Mask:

Ingredients: 1 tablespoon of oatmeal
                     1 tablespoon of cucumber juice

Blend together and make a creamy-smooth paste. Apply it to the face and allow it to dry for twenty minutes or so. Rinse clean with cold water.

To improve oily skin: fold in a teaspoon of fresh lemon juice.

To improve dry skin: fold in a teaspoon of clear honey.

has "given way" in an adult the best plan is to wear a support (which can be bought from any chemist), and to practise foot exercises.

These, although they cannot effect a cure, will give considerable relief, and if the trouble is discovered in its earliest stages will prevent it from developing.

Exercises. 1. Stretch the leg straight out in front, bend it at the ankle, bending the toes backwards.

2. Without moving the foot bend the toes downwards.

3. Keeping the toes still bent downwards stretch out the foot, making the ankle rigid.

4. While keeping the ankle rigid bend the toes upwards.

Breathing Exercise to Develop the Chest. Stand erect, with the shoulders well back, head up and feet about 5 in. apart. Stretch the arms out straight in front, on a level with the shoulders, with the palms of the hands facing each other. Take a deep breath through the nostrils, and with a wide sweeping movement make a large circle, passing the hands as far behind the back as possible.

This exercise is somewhat on the lines of the breast stroke in swimming, and is excellent for chest development.

To improve the Shoulders and Upper Arms. Take a light cane, hold it by the left hand and pass it over the head, grasping it with the right hand while it is poised over the head.

Swing the cane down in front to the level of the waist and pass it up and over the head and down again. Return to original position and repeat.

Skipping is excellent for developing the chest, shoulders, and arms, and the too-thin woman should skip every day for from ten to twenty minutes; but never immediately after a meal or when tired.

Plenty of rest and sleep is essential to those who would put on a little more flesh. From eight to nine hours is not too much, and at least half an hour's rest in the afternoon should be secured. Before taking this rest it is a good plan to sip slowly a glass of warm milk to which a well-beaten egg has been added.

<u>Flushing.</u> Flushing after meals is a sign of a faulty digestion. All food should be carefully masticated, eaten very slowly, and no liquid taken at meal times. Half an hour after finishing, sip, very slowly, a glass of hot water. Indigestible foods such as new bread, pastries, and pork should be avoided.

Often the flushing is confined only to the nose, and when this is the case even more care should be taken to eat only those articles of diet which are easily digested. A little pale-green powder dusted over the nose before the ordinary shade is used will successfully hide any flushing.

Those who suffer in this way should not use any shade of pink powder, for, when the skin beneath it becomes flushed, pink gives a purple tint to the face.

<u>Freckles.</u> The thinner and finer the skin the more liable it is to freckle easily, and those with a skin of this type should endeavour to protect it by applying a little oil of sweet almonds or pure olive oil beneath their complexion powder. The use of the oil will not make the complexion appear greasy. Only a very little is required.

This should be thoroughly rubbed into the pores before the vanishing or "day" cream is put on. After the powder puff has been used there will be no trace of the oil visible, but it will protect the skin from freckles and sunburn.

<u>Gadgets, Beauty.</u> There are several little beauty gadgets which while expensive to buy can

Health & Beauty Monthly

E S S E N T I A L   O I L S

Extract Of Witch-hazel

Witch-hazel is often used on the muscular fibre of veins. The distilled extract from the fresh leaves and twigs is a remedy for the treatment of varicose veins, being applied on a lint bandage, which should be kept moist.

Extract of Witch-hazel is much used as a general remedy for burns, scalds, and inflammatory conditions of the skin.

For insect bites, a pad of cotton-wool, dampened with the extract and applied to the affected spot will help the pain and swelling to subside.

In ointment form it is used externally for piles.

be made at home very inexpensively, and which are of great assistance in giving oneself beauty treatments.

A Massage Roller. A useful massage roller can be made from an ordinary rolling pin. Get a rolling pin from one of the sixpenny stores and a piece of soft chamois leather. Measure the length of the pin exclusive of the handles, and cut a length of the leather to the required size.

Roll the leather round the pin and stick to the roller with strong paste. This roller is excellent for rolling the upper arms, hips, etc., where massage with a roller is more effective than that given by hand.

A "Patter" for a Double Chin. To make a massage "patter" which is excellent for massage when treating a double chin, use a wooden spoon. Place several layers of cotton-wool in the bowl of the spoon to make it quite level with the rim. Make a chamois leather bag to fit over the bowl and fasten it tightly to the handle of the spoon, either sewing or tying it.

DAPHnE'S PATTER'S hAE GUID—BETTER WI' A mUCKLE ROLLIn' PIn!

Use the spoon for patting the space beneath the chin when treating a too-plump neck and chin. Several of these little chamois leather covers, or bags, should be made so that they may be washed when soiled. In this way a most useful little beauty gadget can be made for a few pence.

When applying Mascara. To prevent mascara, or eyebrow pencil, from marking the skin beneath the eyes when the eyelashes are being "made up", take a piece of rather thin white cardboard and cut a small crescent-shaped piece.

Hold this beneath the lashes when using the pencil or applying mascara.

Gooseflesh. Gooseflesh, or Goosebumps may be a temporary condition due to exposure to extreme cold, or, as more often the case, it may be a permanent condition, especially when found on the backs of the arms and legs, owing to impaired circulation.

When it appears on the backs of the arms or legs it has the appearance of pimples beneath the skin, which give a rough, red look to the skin, entirely spoiling the beauty of the arms.

To remedy the condition the circulation must be improved and skin treated externally to remove the roughness. For this get a loofah, soak it in lukewarm water, and soap thickly. Wash the arms or legs, as the case may be, and scrub thoroughly with the soaped loofah. Do not rub hard enough to bruise the skin, but sufficiently so to make it pink and glowing. Rinse off the soap, dry the skin, and massage a little good cold cream into the pores. This treatment will redden the skin at first but the redness will fade away in the course of a few hours and the skin will be much smoother and softer afterwards. Continue with the treatment until a complete cure has been effected, giving it every night or morning as preferred.

Gums. To keep the gums healthy and in good condition they should be massaged every morning with the tip of the finger dipped in a little cold water.

Gums, when "Spongy."
When the gums are "spongy", and they appear to be receding from the teeth, a few drops of myrrh should be added to half a glass of warm water and the mouth rinsed once or twice daily.

Healthy gums are essential to healthy teeth, and any signs of colourlessness or receeding should be treated without delay.

Hair. —The Care of the Hair.
Few and extremely simple are the rules for keeping the hair in good condition. Scalp massage

Healthy Living

Myrrh

MYRRH was burned as an old remedy for getting rid of fleas.

Later it was used as a tonic for people who required to have their strength built up. It was thought to improve circulation and to be an effective decongestant and expectorant in respiratory disease, such as bronchitis, catarrh, colds and tuberculosis. In diseases that involved a rash, myrrh was thought to push the eruption to the surface and speed recovery.

The appetite was thought to be stimulated by it, and it was meant to improve digestion and cure flatulence. It was thought to be effective against intestinal parasites.

Myrrh was used to regulate late periods and was used as a relaxant to relieve spasm. It was also used to induce contractions when childbirth was thought to be imminent, and therefore was not used by pregnant women unless the birth was due.

It was used as a gargle and a mouthwash and to bring relief for minor injuries.

Myrrh was highly prized in the ancient world and has been used since time immemorial as an ingredient in perfumes and incense.

should be given regularly every night, followed by a thorough combing in every direction, and two or three times during the year a tonic should be massaged on to the scalp every night for five or six weeks. A shampoo, suited to the particular needs of the individual hair, should be given every ten days, or at the longest every fortnight. Fair hair requires shampooing every week if it is to remain bright and glossy.

Every spring and autumn the hair falls rather more than at other times, and it is then that a tonic is necessary to check the fall and stimulate the growth.

When massaging the scalp remember that the scalp must be moved. Merely rubbing on the scalp will be of no benefit. A loose scalp is a healthy one, and the hands should be placed firmly on the head, on either side, with the thumb and fourth finger resting on it while the first, second, and third are used for the massage. The whole head should be thoroughly massaged and the tonic dabbed amongst the roots with a pad of cotton-wool.

When the Hair is too Greasy. When the hair is too greasy the scalp should be massaged every night with a few drops of bay rum, and after the massage the hair well ventilated. The best method of ventilating both hair and scalp is by means of combing. Comb the hair from the nape of the neck towards the crown of the head and from the ears right across the head. This should be done night and morning and the hair will look thicker, brighter, and more wavy.

A Tonic for Greasy Hair. Take: 5 drachms of spirits of rosemary; 2 drachms of glycerine of borax; 3 drachms bay rum; 7 oz of water.

Hair that is naturally greasy always appears more so when short, either bobbed or shingled. The reason for this is that the amount of oil secreted by the roots has a smaller quantity of hair over which to spread itself, and the simplest method of removing the grease is by the bay-rum massage advised above.

54

A little of the bay rum should be poured into a small saucer and the fingers dipped into it, from time to time, during the massage. Comb well.

<u>When the Hair is too Dry.</u> When the hair is too dry the massage should be given with oil instead of bay rum. Olive oil or oil of sweet almonds should be chosen, the olive being the less expensive. During the colder months of the year the oil should be slightly warmed before it is used. After the oil massage, comb as after the bay rum.

<u>Waving the Hair.</u> There are types of beauty which look their best with straight locks, but the average woman is improved by a few well-set waves in her hair. Those who have been gifted with wavy hair are in the minority, and the question with which the average woman is faced is "How shall I wave my hair?"

She may have a permanent wave, have it Marcelled, waved with ordinary irons, or water waved. When funds permit most of us prefer a "perm". When properly done this should not harm the hair, and it will last for six months, perhaps a little longer if it is carefully re-set after each shampoo. The newest method of permanent waving, called the Rollair, has introduced a wave which is not only more natural looking but more becoming.

By this method the waving is started at the roots of the hair (formerly it started at the tips) and by starting at the roots the waves are larger nearest the head. This is the way with natural waves, which are always deepest and widest nearest the roots. A head waved by this method gives a perfectly natural appearance — in fact, it is difficult to know whether the hair has been "permed" or not, so natural does it look.

Of waving with irons, the Marcelle is the best method and gives the most attractive-looking results. How long a Marcelle wave will last must depend upon the individual hair and also on the state of the weather— damp, foggy weather will remove almost any wave in a few days.

The ordinary wave with irons is seldom used nowadays. The waves it makes are too small and too close and do not look natural enough to satisfy the modern woman.

What a fuss. Just wear a bonnet!

55

Water-waving is one of the easiest and best methods for the woman whose hair has a natural kink. For this the hair is damped, preferably with a setting lotion, but soft, lukewarm water will answer quite well, and the hair set in waves by means of small combs called "setting combs". After fixing the combs into position a shingle cap should be slipped on and worn till the hair is quite dry. Comb out after an hour or longer. Hair that has been water-waved should not be combed out immediately the combs are removed if the wave is to last for more than a few hours.

To deepen or re-set a wave, rub the head over with a damp towel, or hold it near a steaming kettle, for a few minutes, and press into waves, using an old silk handkerchief folded like a pad. Should the hair need a gloss, massage a few drops of oil into the scalp and comb through before starting to re-set the wave.

<u>To Wave the Hair.</u> Separate the whites from the yolk of one egg. Whisk the white and mix it with ½ pint of cold, soft water, add a few drops of perfume, and bottle. Apply a little of this to the hair before arranging waves or curls.

Rosewater may be used instead of ordinary soft water, and in that case no perfume will be required.

<u>Hair colours, what will suit you?</u> The woman who understands making the best of herself will not wear a colour because it is fashionable or because one of her friends looks well in it. She will test the colour for herself.

A famous dressmaker gives as the best method of discovering whether a shade will suit one or not, is by draping it around the neck and head. If the colour deepens that of the eyes, the shade should be worn, but if it makes the eyes look pale and colourless it should be discarded, no matter how attractive it may be in itself.

<u>What the Blonde may Wear.</u> The ash-blonde should avoid all shades of orange, bright red, any tone of yellow, and the fashionable colour called "henna".

She may wear with success cream, white, soft greens, all shades pale blue, and all tones of grey, particularly the French grey and soft silver shades.

The Golden Blonde can wear black as well as white, rose, pale shades of yellow, and all the lighter shades of brown.

Brunettes of pale colouring can also wear both black and white and olive greens, with some shades of blue, dark red, tan, and most shades of brown.

The Brunette with very vivid colouring will be striking in black, especially if she has a good skin, and bright greens will also suit her. Orange and all shades of yellow and flame, golden brown and tan. She should avoid pink and very pale shades.

The Woman who is Betwixt and Between, if she has a good complexion, has a very wide field of choice. Almost any shade will suit her, and if she is not quite certain of it, she can try the method of draping it around her before finally deciding that which is suggested above.

The Auburn-haired looks her best in black and coppery shades, emerald green, and gold.

Silvery Hair always looks particularly distinguished in black, black and white, silvery grey, and shades of lavender, also pale shades of mauve.

Hair

There were several traditional treatments for improving the condition of the hair. Washing the hair with egg was one of these, and castor oil was another well-known hair conditioner.

Applying an infusion of fresh nettle leaves was meant to have a beneficial effect on the hair. Fresh parsley juice was thought to make the hair shiny, and a decoction of burdock was massaged into the scalp as a hair tonic.

An infusion of camomile flowers was meant to be an effective hair tonic, the scalp being cleansed with it twice a week. Another infusion made with sage, rosemary, honeysuckle and plantain with added honey was used as a hair wash to improve the condition of the hair. A strong infusion of sage alone was recommended as a hair tonic, and this was also meant to cure dandruff.

Hair fall was frequently treated with folk remedies. Again, egg was recommended. Fresh eggs were to be beaten, rubbed into the hair and left overnight. Damping the hair with an infusion of sage was also said to help prevent hair falling out.

Dilute rosemary oil rubbed on the scalp was also meant to stop hair falling out, and castor oil applied in the same way was also meant to be effective. A rinse made from yarrow was also used to prevent hair fall, and a mixture of boxwood, rosemary and marshmallow added to boiling water had the same claims made for it.

A mixture of kerosene and water used in equal parts was used in the cure of dandruff but it was also claimed to be able to stop the hair from growing grey if it was applied early enough.

24

Tonics for the Hair.—Tonic Oil for Massaging the Scalp. Take 2 oz. of deodorised castor oil, 2 oz. of coconut oil, and 1 oz. of oil of rosemary.

Mix and heat gently, shaking till all are thoroughly blended, adding, while shaking, a ½ drachm of oil of jasmine.

A Tonic for Dry Hair. Take: tincture of cantharides, 4 drachms; spirits of rosemary, 4 drachms; dilute acetic acid, 3 drachms; bay rum, 3 drachms; water to make 7 oz. Mix and apply to the scalp with massage.

A Hair Tonic for stimulating Growth. Take 4 drachms of tincture of cantharides, 4 drachms of spirits of rosemary, dilute 3 drachms of acetic acid, 3 drachms bay rum, 7 oz. of water. Mix and massage into the scalp every night.

Greyness, Premature. Premature greyness is often hereditary, occasionally it is due to shock or general nervous conditions. Generally, massage given to the scalp every night and morning and taking an iron tonic will help to arrest it, but sometimes nothing appears to do any good. The only way is to try several different remedies and note which gives the best results.

Massage, however, should never be omitted from the treatment, for by stimulating the tiny blood vessels beneath the scalp the colour cells will be greatly benefited. The following tonic, applied every night, will be of help when the greyness is due to nervous conditions or shock.

The Tonic.—Take 1 oz. of tincture of jaborandi; 15 grains of sulphate of quinine; 1 oz. of glycerine; 4 oz. of bay rum; 10 oz. of distilled water. Mix and apply to the roots of the hair after thoroughly massaging the scalp. Should all these methods fail there is nothing to be done, except use a tint or dye. The hair should be given plenty of light and air, for ventilation is of as great importance in preserving the colour as in maintaining the general health of the hair.

Silver Hair, the Care of. Silver hair requires special care to prevent it from becoming yellowish. It should be shampooed every week, dried by fanning, and no oils allowed to come into contact with it. A little liquid (toilet) paraffin may be massaged into the roots before brushing.

<u>Curling Fluids.</u> When the hair has a natural kink no curling fluid should be necessary, and it will be ample to shake a comb out in water, pass it through the hair, and pinch the waves into position with the fingers. But straight hair, and hair that is artificially waved, or curled, whether "permed" or Marcelled, needs a curling fluid to help it to set in correct waves.

A good curling fluid may be bought from any hairdresser, but those who would like to make one at home can do so from the following recipe:

Dissolve ½ drachm of gum arabic and 1 oz. of borax in a pint of boiling water, and when dissolved add 1 oz. of spirits of camphor. Bottle, and apply to the hair with a spray. An excellent curling fluid for use in emergency can be made by dissolving a lump of sugar in a small coffee cup of hot water. This mixture is excellent for fixing little "kiss" curls.

<u>Dandruff.</u> Dandruff is of two kinds—the dry and the greasy. The former is the more common form and should never be allowed to remain unchecked, as dandruff permitted to stay on the scalp causes the hair to lose its vitality and fall, and induces premature greyness.

To remove dry dandruff give the head an oil-bath. For this, get some olive oil (only the best quality should be used), warm it slightly by standing the bottle in a bowl of hot, not boiling, water. Part the hair every half-inch and, with a pad of cotton-wool, apply the oil liberally to the scalp and roots of the hair. Wrap the head in a warm towel and leave for three or four hours, according to the condition of the scalp. The more dandruff there is, the longer the oil should be allowed to soak into the roots. Shampoo off, using a pine-tar shampoo and dry the hair by fanning and with warm towels, but never before a fire.

Unless the scalp is in a very bad condition one treatment should entirely remove the dandruff, but if it does not, give another about a week after the first.

Those who suffer with dandruff should be very careful in the choice of combs and brushes used. These should not be hard or the combs sharp enough to irritate the scalp, and they should be washed with a mild antiseptic lotion every day.

The scalp should be dabbed occasionally with a weak boric lotion to which a few drops of spirits of camphor have been added.

After the oil-bath a tonic lotion to stimulate the growth of the hair should be applied regularly every night till an improvement has been effected.

When brushing or combing hair that is troubled with dandruff, it ought always to be treated gently, as, if pulled roughly, there is every probability that it will fall considerably. A tonic, such as one of iron or hypophosphites, should be taken to tone up the general system.

For greasy dandruff the following lotion will be found beneficial: Resorcin, 20 grains; surgical spirit, 2 drachms; water, 2 oz. To be dabbed amongst the roots of the hair.

<u>Hair.—Tonic for Use after removing Dandruff.</u> Hair that has suffered with dandruff needs a good tonic. First remove the dandruff with an oil bath, shampoo with a pine-tar shampoo, and apply the following tonic every night for four or five weeks, or longer if the hair is in a very impoverished condition.

Take: 2 drachms of castor oil; 4 ozs. of surgical spirit; 5 grains sulphate of quinine; ½ oz. of lavender water

Mix and apply to the scalp after thoroughly massaging the whole head.

The following astringent lotion should also be applied in the morning, after giving the hair a good combing: 2 drachms spirits of camphor; 3 drachms of glycerine of borax; 1 oz. spirits of rosemary; 7 ozs. orangeflower water.

A little to be rubbed into the scalp about once every week.

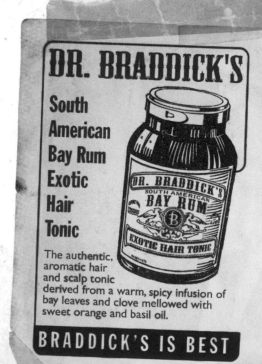

Brilliantine, for the Hair. To give a gloss to the hair it should be brushed with a perfectly clean brush, sprinkled with a few drops of brilliantine, using golden brilliantine for fair or light-brown hair, and henna brilliantine for reddish-brown or auburn. Almost every chemist and hairdresser will supply brilliantine in these shades. After the brushing take an old silk handkerchief, fold it like a pad, and brush the hair with it, pressing the waves in the hair into position. This silk pad gives a better gloss than any brush and its use helps to deepen the waves and makes them remain in the hair longer. It is an excellent treatment for the hair when dressing for a dance or other entertainment.

SERIES 2

Dr. FARQUHARSON'S

HERBAL HOME CURES

Castor Oil

Castor oil is one of the oldest remedies known, and it has been used as a laxative for thousands of years. It has a particularly unpleasant odour and taste and so is difficult to take. One old remedy suggests floating it on hot milk and eating a piece of orange or lemon peel before taking it. Alternatively, something with a strong taste, such as peppermint, could be taken before, with, or after it.

Externally castor oil was used as a hair conditioner and as a remedy for dandruff and hair fall. It was also thought to be effective in treating irritation caused by the presence of a foreign body in the eye.

Dyes, Hair. The question of dyeing the hair when its natural colour begins to fade is one which should be approached with caution. Once a dye is started it must be continued and the same preparation used. As the hair grows the new portion, along the roots, appears white or grey as the case may be, and this portion must be touched up again and again as it lengthens. In fact, dyed hair must be "touched up" every fortnight if the fact that it is dyed is not to be proclaimed to the whole world.

Almost every dye contains some poisonous ingredient, and although this may not take effect the first time the dye is applied, should there be a scratch on the scalp or the user rather "run down" poisoning may be set up with disastrous results.

If grey hair is not becoming or is considered ageing the safest and best plan is to use one of the vegetable preparations and tint the hair. Henna is excellent for reddish or reddish-brown hair, and camomile for fair or light brown. Henna gives warm, red-gold tints and camomile pretty golden lights.

<u>To apply Henna.</u> Henna may be applied either in liquid or paste form, the latter being the easier. For this get henna powder. Shampoo the hair and dry it so that it may be entirely free from grease either natural or applied. Mix the henna powder to a paste with boiling water and, with a brush, apply the paste to the hair, dividing it in strands and spreading the paste right along the hair from the roots to the ends.

When the whole head has been treated wrap it in a towel and leave from half an hour to one hour according to the depth of colour required. Shampoo off. Follow with a good brushing with a brush smeared with a few drops of brilliantine. A little oil massaged into the scalp the night after the henna application has been given will be beneficial, for henna is very drying to the hair.

When a liquid application is preferred the henna leaves must be obtained. These are boiled with a small lump of soda and the liquid strained and then applied to the hair. A liquid henna application is to be preferred when the hair is very thick, but in every other case the paste will be found simpler and more easily applied.

<u>To Tint Dark Hair.</u> A mixture of one part castor oil and three parts bay rum brushed through the hair will often disguise greyness most satisfactorily and gives a pretty gloss at the same time. The oil and bay rum should be well shaken every time the mixture is applied, for oil and spirits do not blend well.

<u>General Rules for Dyeing the Hair.</u> The hair must be shampooed and dried in every case before a dye is applied.

The dye should be tested on a small portion of the hair before being applied to the whole head.

Any touch of dye which may come into contact with the forehead or throat should be removed with a little cream immediately it is noticed, otherwise the skin will be stained.

It is advisable to wear a pair of rubber gloves when applying the dye. This prevents staining the hands or finger-nails from which it is always difficult to remove dye of any sort.

Oil or brilliantine should be brushed through the hair when the dye has thoroughly dried. Besides giving a gloss this treatment helps set the dye.

<u>Henna.</u> Henna is used largely in the East for giving reddish tints to the hair. It is not injurious and is therefore a favourite medium for tinting hair that is fading or turning grey. It can be used either as paste or lotion and should be applied to the hair while quite hot.

<u>Setting Lotion for the Hair.</u> Dissolve 1 drachm of gum arabic in 2 oz. of boiling water. Place this in an 8-oz. bottle. Add ½ an oz. of powdered borax and shake till dissolved. A few drops of perfume may be added if desired.

<u>Shampoo, how to.</u> Before starting to shampoo the hair pass a comb through it and damp it thoroughly with warm water. When a shampoo powder is used, divide the powder into two separate portions.

Use one, and after rinsing the hair in two separate waters, shampoo a second time, using the other portion of the powder. This is the professional way of shampooing, and it will give the best results. Plenty of water should be used for rinsing, and when a spray is not available the last rinsing water can be poured over the head from a small watering-can.

Never dry the hair before a fire.

Warm towels should be used to squeeze out as much water as possible, and the drying finished by fanning with a palm-leaf fan.

Very dry hair will be much benefited if a little oil is well massaged into the scalp the night before the shampoo.

No ammonia should ever be added to a shampoo, for although it helps to brighten the hair it is too drying and is very injurious to both the roots and scalp.

<u>Shampoos.—For the Blonde.</u> Take about ⅓ of a cake of white Castile soap and shred it finely. Place in 1 pint of soft water and stand on the stove till the soap jellies. Allow to become cool. Beat the yolks only of 2 eggs, with a teaspoonful of good eau-de-Cologne, and add to the soap

66

jelly. Beat again, adding a little lukewarm water till the whole is well mixed.

Damp the hair with warm water and shampoo the soap mixture well into the scalp and roots. Rinse off with clear warm water. To brighten the hair give a camomile rinse as a third and last rinsing water. For this put 1 oz. of camomile flowers into a large jug, pour over them one pint of boiling water, stir, and cover the jug; allow to stand fifteen minutes, and use as a rinse.

For Dark Hair. Shave the same quantity of Castile soap into 1 pint of boiling water and beat till it jellies. When cool add ½ a teaspoonful of powdered borax and 2 tablespoonfuls of bay rum. Beat together and shampoo into the hair in the usual way. Rinse in three separate waters, adding to the last rinsing a tablespoonful of white wine vinegar.

Dry Shampoo. Mix together 2 oz. of the best cornflour and 1 of powdered orrisroot. Pass through a fine sieve. Sprinkle the powder over the scalp and hair; allow to remain on for a few minutes, brush out with a clean brush.

The brush for use with a dry shampoo must be perfectly dry and free from any trace of grease.

For Silvery Hair. Take the whites of 3 eggs and beat them together with a teaspoonful of powdered borax and 3 tablespoonfuls of hot water.

When well beaten add gradually ½ a pint of hot water, and shampoo through the hair. Rinse in three separate waters.

<u>Superfluous Hair.</u> Superfluous hair is one of the greatest difficulties with which the modern beauty doctor has to contend. It can be removed temporarily by depilatories, or it may be bleached with peroxide of hydrogen. The only permanent method of removing it is by electrolysis.

Those with a tendency towards superfluous hair should be extremely careful in the choice of toilet preparation, soaps, creams, etc. No cream should be allowed to remain (during the night) on those parts of the face where a growth of hair might appear and after using cream on the upper lip, chin, etc., it should be wiped off and an astringent lotion dabbed over the skin. Superfluous hair on the arms and legs is best removed by shaving.

<u>Hands, the Care of the.</u> To keep the hands soft, white, and smooth is not difficult, even the woman who must attend to her own household duties can have well-kept hands with very little trouble. Always cleanse the hands in lukewarm water, softened with some borax or good bath salts, and dry them thoroughly. Half-dried hands result in roughness and chaps in winter and a coarse skin in summer. Keep a bottle of glycerine and rosewater handy, and when the hands are half dried pour 2 or 3 drops of the mixture into the palm of the hand and rub it over them as if washing them. Finish drying and dust over with a mixture of fine oatmeal and powdered orris root, 1 part of the orris root to 4 of the oatmeal. The mixture should be passed through a fine sieve and put into a jar with a wide mouth and well-fitted lid.

The orris root gives a dainty suggestion of violets to the mixture, which can be increased by adding a few drops of essence of violets to the oatmeal.

<u>Old, Wrinkled Hands.</u> When the hands look dried, wrinkled, and old, they should be fed regularly with warm olive oil or oil of sweet almonds. This condition is often due to extreme dryness of the skin, not from the passing of the years.

Plunging the hands into very hot water is another cause, and the woman who does her own housework often makes her hands old and wrinkled by using soda for washing up and other household duties. In place of soda use a little borax for softening the water. It is quite as effective and will not injure the hands. Also use a mop for washing crockery and rubber gloves for any other occasions when the hands must be placed in water.

Every night warm some oil — olive or oil of almonds — and, after thoroughly cleansing the hands, rub the oil well into the skin. Apply as much as the pores will absorb, allow it to soak well in and slip on a pair of old, loose-fitting gloves, wearing them till next morning. Even a week of these oil baths will show a great improvement.

Never half wash the hands. If gardening or other work has soiled them badly, put some oil or cream in the palms and rub it well into the skin, especially over the knuckles and palms. Wipe off the grease with an old piece of soft muslin or a piece of tissue-paper and wash in warm water, using a good superfatted soap.

To Whiten the Hands. Mix together a tablespoonful of oil of sweet almonds and one of rosewater. Beat up the yolk of an egg and add to the oil and water and beat together, adding, a drop at a time, 50 drops of simple tincture of benzoin.

This mixture should be spread over the hands at night after cleansing them with soft warm water and soap, and a pair of gloves worn till next morning.

Gloves for sleeping should always have a hole cut in the palms to allow of ventilation.

A Cream to whiten the Hands. Take 2 drachms of spermaceti, 1 drachm of liquid paraffin, 1 oz. of lanolin, 3 oz. of olive oil, 5 grains of powdered borax, ½ an oz. of rosewater. Melt the spermaceti and lanolin, stir in the paraffin and olive oil, and beat thoroughly. Add the borax and

ORRIS ROOT (Iris germanica)
This herb was chiefly used for chest complaints and as a purgative. It is diuretic and can be used for dropsy and other water retention problems, colic and liver congestion. It is now most commonly used as a fixative in potpourris and perfumes, due to its sweet smell. It is an excellent way to brush your teeth and will strengthen your gums, and freshen the breath. Orris Root Powder can be used as snuff to bring on sneezing when having headache congestion. Dosage or Use: Take ½ to 1 Teaspoons in juice or tea. Or as directed.

beat again; heat the rosewater and add this last of all, beating the mixture to a cream till quite cold. Unless thoroughly beaten this cream will not mix well; the rosewater will become separated from the other ingredients.

Cucumber Cream. Take 2 cucumbers and slice them without peeling. Put them in 4 oz. of olive oil and leave them for twenty-four hours. Press the cucumbers to a pulp in the oil and strain through a fine sieve. Melt 2 oz. of lanolin, 2 drachms. of white wax, and 1 drachm of spermaceti. Add the strained cucumber oil and beat to a cream, adding 3 drops of essence of violets to scent. This may be omitted if preferred.

Honey Cream for the Hands. Put 4 oz. of honey and 1 oz. of glycerine in a jar and heat gently; add 1 drachm of citric acid and 1 oz. of surgical spirit with 6 drops of essence of verbena.

Shake well, and always shake before using. The honey and glycerine, after being blended, should be allowed to cool before the other ingredients are added.

An Inexpensive Cold Cream. Take ½ a lb. of the best lard and put it in a basin. Pour over it sufficient hot water to cover; the water should be almost boiling. Leave till cold and repeat the process till the lard has been melted 3 times. Put it in a clean basin, add 2 tablespoonfuls of rosewater, and beat into the lard, adding a few drops of any perfume desired.

Too Thin Hands, with Prominent Veins. When the hands are too thin and the veins show up too prominently it gives them an old, worn look. For this, massage with a little cocoa butter is the best remedy.

Get a stick of cocoa butter and rub the hands with it immediately they have been washed in warm water, and while the skin is still warm. Cocoa butter is very hard in the stick in which it generally is sold, but as soon as it comes into contact with the skin it melts quite easily, and it is an excellent feeding agent for the hands.

Massage the hands gently across the backs from the base of the fingers towards the wrist. This will reduce the too-prominent veins.

Glycerine does not agree with every skin, but when it does it is

70

excellent for softening and whitening the hands. Before much is used a little should be tried on the back of one of the hands. If it makes the skin red and smart do not use it, for that is a sign that it does not suit your particular type of skin.

Treatment for Moist Hands. During the summer months some women suffer with very moist hands, which are not only uncomfortable but tend to spoil the work done, especially if it is fancy work or fine needlework.

To remedy the condition bathe the hands with a mixture of alum and water, half a teaspoonful of alum to half a pint of water. Dissolve the alum in water, and bottle for use when required. Dip a piece of cotton-wool in the mixture and dab over the palms and fingers. Allow to dry on and dust the hands with a little of the following powder:

2 ozs. of powdered orris root; 4 ozs. of fine oatmeal and 1 drachm of oil of bergamot. Mix thoroughly and keep in a tin with a perforated lid.

Haresfoot. A haresfoot should find a place on every woman's dressing-table. It is the very best form of powder-puff for giving the finishing touches to the complexion. After powdering take the haresfoot and "dust" over the face. This gives a very smooth "matt" look to the skin and prevents the powder from looking patchy.

A haresfoot can be bought at any chemist and the price is quite small. A mounted one would cost about half a crown; unmounted one shilling.

Headache. Bathing the back of the neck and immediately behind the ears with a sponge dipped in very hot water will often relieve a

H - HEADACHE

headache

An old English superstition held that hair that had either been cut from the head or that had fallen out of its own accord was not to be thrown away in a careless manner. If the hair was carelessly discarded, the fear was that a bird would find the hair and carry it off and use it for nest-building. Apparently, if this happened the head of the owner of the hair would ache all the time that the bird was building the nest. There were several folk remedies for headaches. An infusion made from elderflowers was held to be a cure, as was an infusion of lime flowers, an infusion of dried rosemary or an infusion of camomile. A tea made from betony was also regarded as curative.

The Greeks and Romans used peppermint as a cure for headaches. Later, cures taken internally included cinnamon, honey, and apple. Rosemary, camomile, dock, lavender, balm and meadowsweet were herbs that were taken internally as a cure.

Joe swallaes a bottle o' ginger when he has a sair heid!

headache, especially when it is of nervous origin. A short rest in a darkened room, after the bathing, will generally effect a cure. When headaches are persistent, and especially when they are early morning headaches, it is a sign of liver trouble, and liver pills taken at night with the addition of a cup of camomile tea will often effect a complete cure. Headaches should never be neglected by the woman who studies her appearance, for they make the eyes look dull and heavy, and hair never waves or "sets" well on an aching head.

Calamine *is used in the form of a cream or a lotion. It has a cooling, calming and soothing effect on the skin for the symptomatic relief of itching. With the active ingredient zinc oxide, which has antiseptic properties it helps prevent infection from scratching. Calamine is a part of a class of medicines called the anti-pruritics, which are identified as relieving itching caused by chemical changes in the skin or some physical irritation caused by disease, inflammation, allergic reaction, the side-effects of some medical application, or reaction to any irritant substances.*

Heat Spots. Heat spots and heat rashes are generally the result of drinking cold liquids when overheated. It is best when very hot, and at the same time very thirsty, to take tea instead of cold drinks, and sip it very slowly. A little calamine lotion mopped over the spots will help to cure them, but even if left entirely alone they will generally disappear after a very few hours have elapsed.

Honey for Beauty. Honey is quite invaluable as a toilet article. If a small jar is kept in the bathroom or on the dressing-table it will be useful for rubbing into rough, chapped hands during wintry weather, and for soothing chapped lips.

It helps to soften and whiten the skin, and when mixed with half its quantity of rose or orange-flower water, makes the hands very soft and white. It should be rubbed into the skin when they are half dry, and the drying finished with a soft towel.

Indigestion. Indigestion is a great foe to beauty. It makes the complexion rough, gives pimples and blotches, a flushed face, and every often a red nose. Those who suffer with digestive troubles should avoid strong tea, new bread, pastries, and potatoes, also pork and fatty meats, which are always difficult to digest. Meals should be small and light, the greatest nourishment in the smallest bulk. All food should be eaten slowly, no exercise taken immediately after a meal, and a soda mint tablet dissolved in the mouth when there is any feeling of discomfort. A charcoal biscuit, eaten after the two chief meals of the day, will also help.

Insomnia. Insomnia or sleeplessness is another beauty destroyer. Sufficient sound sleep is essential for preserving the complexion, preventing wrinkles, and keeping the eyes bright and clear. Those who suffer with insomnia will find that a glass of warm milk, slowly sipped the last thing at night, will be a great help in inducing sleep.

A walk in the fresh air just before going to bed is another means of inducing sleep that should be tried by all who are troubled in this way. Sleeping draughts should not be taken till every other means have been tried without success, and then only under doctor's orders.

Placing the bed so that the head is to the north is said to be a means of inducing sound sleep, and this method has been tried, and found successful, by several sufferers from lack of ability to obtain restful sleep.

Knees. Very few women possess beautiful knees. When a woman is very thin her knees are too bony and pointed for beauty; when she is fat they are too large and heavy. Stair climbing is excellent for improving the shape of the knees, and practising the old-fashioned curtsey also helps.

honey

HONEY was thought to be highly nutritious and was particularly recommended for people who had been ill to give them energy. A remedy advocated for delicate children consisted of boiled milk with added honey.

It was also used as a sedative and to promote relaxation and sleep, and as such was sometimes used in cases of insomnia. Again, it was sometimes added to hot milk and taken just before going to bed.

Honey was considered to be a very versatile substance in folk medicine. It was, for example, thought to relieve the pain of headaches, neuralgia or arthritis.

It was frequently used as an expectorant and was helpful in the treatment of coughs and catarrh. It was sometimes used with hot lemon to soothe sore throats, and is often used in this way today. Herbs, such as thyme, were sometimes added to it to relieve the symptoms of asthma or bronchitis. Honey was thought to have the power to relieve congestion, and was used in the treatment of sinusitis, and hay fever.

Diarrhoea and vomiting were treated with it, and it was thought to help in the treatment of various infections, such as typhoid.

Externally, honey was used as a treatment for burns and as a means of bringing boils to a head. It was also thought to speed up the cure of sores or ulcers in the mouth. Wounds were once spread with honey in the belief that it would aid healing.

In early times honey was regarded as an aphrodisiac.

20

When too thin, the knees can be made more attractive by massage with a few drops of olive oil. This is also excellent for those who suffer with any form of rheumatism or stiffness. When too fat they can be reduced by massage with a mixture of equal parts of spirits of camphor and distilled water.

<u>Lemons for Beauty.</u> A penny lemon is a great aid to beauty. The juice, diluted with an equal quantity of rosewater, makes an excellent bleach for a discoloured neck; equal quantities of lemon juice and rosewater and glycerine will whiten red, rough hands; the juice of a lemon added to the last rinsing water when shampooing the hair makes it bright and glossy and removes all traces of soap or shampoo powder, leaving it shining and smooth and very easy to wave.

The juice of a lemon in a glass of hot water, taken the first thing in the morning, helps to reduce weight. It will clear the complexion of any yellow tinge. It is also excellent for those inclined to be bilious.

Used on the finger-nails it will remove stains, and applied to the cuticle on an orange stick it will act as a cuticle remover.

<u>Lips, the Care of.</u> To keep the lips soft and smooth, and free from ageing wrinkles, they should be massaged every night with the tip of the

finger moistened with a drop of pure glycerine. When a lipstick is not used a little of the glycerine should be applied every morning and always before going into the cold air.

Once allowed to become cracked and blackened it is very difficult to get the lips in good condition again, and besides being unsightly, rough cracked lips are very uncomfortable. Those who do not care to use a coloured lipstick can obtain a white lipstick, which will keep the lips in good condition without giving a "made-up" appearance.

Any chemist will supply a colourless lipstick.

"Make-up", the Art of. A successful "make-up" depends upon the choice of the right preparations, in the shades which will suit the individual colouring, and upon a good foundation. A rough, blotchy skin never "makes-up" well. The skin may be sallow, but it must be smooth and free from enlarged pores. When the skin is coarse and the pores enlarged, powder and rouge sink into them and give the face a patchy look which is very unbecoming.

Before starting to make-up, thoroughly cleanse the face, and if it is the second "make-up" that day remove all cream and powder previously used. Nothing spoils the skin more than to pile "make-up" on a soiled foundation, and even if the powder and cream have only been on the face a few hours it is sure to be slightly soiled.

If you have a very dry skin it is best to use as a

foundation a form of cold cream; vanishing creams are more suited to the greasy skin. Very little is required of whichever is chosen, and it must be spread very evenly over the face and neck. Put a tiny dab on each cheek, one on the chin, and one on the forehead, with another on the nose. Work these little dabs of cream well into the skin, but avoid putting any of the cream on the upper lip.

Next apply your rouge. This should be a cream rouge if the skin is dry; in any case it is always the easier to apply, for the edges can be softened more easily than when a powder is employed.

The edges of the rouge, whether cream or powder variety, must be softened and blended into the cream, for hard edges give away the fact that the face is rouged and are very inartistic.

After applying the rouge, put on your powder. It is best to apply this with a pad of cotton-wool, and it should not be rubbed on. Be generous with it and apply it with little pats, going over the whole face. Leave a thick layer on the face while the eyebrows, eyelashes, and lips are attended to, then dust off, using a haresfoot. This will leave the skin beautifully soft and smooth and with that much coveted "matt" appearance.

With a small brush remove all powder from the eyebrows, brushing them first upwards from the eyes then straight across. When the eyebrows do not require darkening, a drop of brilliantine should be put on the brush; if to be darkened this must be omitted. For darkening the eyebrows and eyelashes, use mascara. Moisten the brush and brush the eyelashes upwards and those on the lower lids downwards. Brush the eyebrows very lightly with the brush used for the eyelashes, but do this very carefully so that the mascara does not stain the skin.

When making up the lips remember that the shape of the mouth can be slightly improved. If the lips are too thin carry the colour a shade beyond the natural line; if too thick do not carry it to the extreme edge of the lips. Put a dab of the lipstick in the centre of each lip and work it towards the corners. A very large mouth should not have the colour carried

to the extreme edge; one that is too small should be rouged from end to end.

When making-up the face remember to treat the neck. A slightly lighter shade of powder can be used on the throat, and it should be as carefully creamed as the face. Often a liquid powder is found more advisable for the throat, and if this is used it should be lightly rubbed over with a piece of chamois leather instead of using the haresfoot.

Every woman should keep two or three shades of powder on her dressing-table — one in a light shade of ochre for dusting the nose when the whole make-up has been completed. A dust of ochre powder on the nose will prevent that white over-powdered look one so often sees and which spoils the whole effect of the make-up no matter how good it may otherwise be.

Manicure. To give the nails a professional manicure you will require a sharp pair of nail scissors, preferably curved, a nail file, a box of emery boards, and a bundle of orange sticks, some polishing paste or varnish, as preferred, and a "buffer".

Before starting operations the tips of the fingers should be soaked in warm soapy water to soften the cuticle at the base of the nail. Then dry the hands and file the nails. When filing remember to work towards the centre of the nail, never outwards. Pointed nails are neither in good taste nor practicable, for they invariably break off or split.

The shape should follow the line of the tip of the finger, and may be a degree beyond the tip of the finger, and a trifle more pointed than the finger, if the fingers are inclined to be spatulate or square. This makes the hands appear a better shape.

Next attend to the cuticle which grows around the base of the nails. The little half-moon which appears at the base of the nail is not always present in every finger, and it must be induced by careful attention to show itself. For a finger that shows the half-moon distinctly at the base of the nail is always much prettier than one which does not.

Dip an orange stick in the soapy water and very gently raise the cuticle around the base of each nail so that it is quite loose. Never cut the cuticle around the base of the nails. Cutting makes it hard and coarse, and causes "hang-nails", which are not only unsightly but also very painful.

The cuticle can be removed with a little liquid cuticle-remover. Wrap a scrap of cotton wool round an orange stick and dip in the cuticle-remover. Work this around the cuticle and leave for a minute or two. Dip the fingers in warm water and rub with a soft towel. The cuticle will disappear, leaving the base of the nail in perfect condition.

Health & Beauty Monthly

E S S E N T I A L   O I L S
**LAVENDAR or
YLANG YLANG CREAM**

1 cup of glycerin
1 cup of rosewater
10 drops of essential oil fragrance,
(lavender or ylang ylang)
¼ teaspoon of vitamin E oil

Put all of the ingredients into a glass bottle. Shake well until all have been combined together. Shake before using.

Dry the fingers and polish the nails. A polishing paste, a stone, or a powder can be used for this, or one of the newer varnishes. When a varnish is used, the old varnish must be removed with a preparation specially prepared for the purpose before more is applied.

Varnish is put up in different colours: pale pink, deep rose, and blood red; the latter is by no means attractive though often seen. It gives to the nails the appearance of dripping talons, which is rather repulsive, and a deep shade of pink is far more artistic. In addition to these there is a silver varnish, and one in shades of mother-of-pearl, which is very dainty, but for all practical purposes the deep pink is to be preferred.

The "buffer" is not required when varnish is used, for this is painted on the nail with a fine brush, but for powder, paste, or a polishing stone the buffer is used to give a final polish.

Massage. Massage forms an important parts of Beauty Culture. It is used for reducing superfluous flesh, for filling out a too-thin figure, for removing wrinkles and lines, and treating hair and scalp troubles.

For reducing flesh, massage should be very hard and firm; for increasing it the touch must be light and gentle, the skin being lightly pinched and kneaded. There is also "tapoment", a light tapping movement given with the balls of the fingers, which is excellent for rounding out a too—thin neck or removing hollows on the throat.

Before massaging for increasing flesh the skin should be bathed with warm water and lightly dried. This is to make it more receptive to the cream which is used in massage.

A general rule to remember when massaging is that all movements should be upwards and outwards for facial treatments, and also upwards towards the body when massaging the legs. When massaging the arms work from the elbows towards the shoulders and from the wrists towards the elbows.

For reducing the back, the massage should be given with a circular movement, pinching and kneading the flesh with hard, firm movements. No cream of any sort should be used when massaging for reducing flesh.

Milk. Milk must be reckoned amongst beauty foods. It is beneficial to the complexion both when taken internally and when used for bathing the skin.

Milk should always be sipped very slowly; when drunk straight off it is apt to become indigestible. It is more beneficial for filling out the figure when taken warm than cold.

For bathing the skin it is excellent, making it soft and white. Buttermilk is wonderful as a bleach of the skin, but it must be fresh to be of any use.

Milk of Almonds. To make milk of almonds to soften and whiten the skin, place 30 almonds in a mortar and bruise, add half a pint of distilled water and beat together, adding a lump of sugar to prevent the oil separating from the water. Bottle and cork tightly.

Rubbed over the hands this lotion has a softening and whitening effect.

mole!

Moles. Moles have often been termed beauty spots, and when they are situated at the corner of the mouth or near the outer corner of the eye they can be very attractive.

If not quite dark enough, they can be darkened by lightly touching with an eyebrow pencil. It is never wise to try and remove a mole, for often in the attempt a scar is made far more disfiguring than the mole could ever be. When one appears on some part of the face which is unbecoming, such as the nose, it should be removed by a doctor, but unless it is really very unsightly it is far better to leave it alone.

Motorist, Beauty for the. Nothing is more trying to the complexion than motoring, especially during windy or very cold weather. Before starting out, the motorist who would keep her skin in perfect condition, should give it a generous coating of good cold cream. Let this sink into the skin for several minutes, wipe off any superfluous grease, and dust with powder.

After a "spin" the face should not be cleansed with soap and water. With a clean soft towel or a piece of cotton-wool remove all the powder and cream, apply a little more cream, and wipe this off also. After this thorough cleansing a little ordinary vanishing cream can be put on and the face powdered as usual.

After a long motor journey give the eyes a bath of warm boric acid lotion. The bath will remove all dust which may have settled in the corners of the eyes or on the roots of the lashes. To allow dust of any sort to remain on the lashes will cause them to weaken and fall out.

Also give the hair a thorough brushing. Even when a really close-fitting cap is worn, the dust from the roads will settle on the hair and rob it of its bright sheen if it is not promptly brushed out.

Mouth, the Care of the. The actual shape of the mouth cannot be altered, but by massage, and training the muscles, and keeping the lips in good condition, its appearance can be much improved.

Biting the lips will quickly ruin the most beautiful mouth, and this habit once acquired is very difficult to break. Occasionally it is done intentionally to bring a colour to the lips, but more often it is due to nervousness. The mouth should never be allowed to remain partly open, this gives a vacant, stupid expression to the whole face.

Close the lips firmly but not tightly, and if the mouth appears to be settling into a discontented droop practise a few mouth exercises. In our grandmothers' days young girls were taught to say "prunes" and "prisms" to improve the shape of the mouth, and much can be done to improve an ugly mouth by whistling and blowing imaginary bubbles as, as advised for the treatment of hollow cheeks.

Nails, Brittle. When the nails are brittle and break off easily it is generally a sign of a tendency to gout. The hands should never be placed in very hot water, and before being washed a drop of oil should be rubbed into them.

Every night they should be soaked in warm olive oil. File, instead of cutting them, and do not keep them long. When the nails are long they are more liable to split and break. Keep them filed close to the tip of the finger.

Nails, Spots on. Spots on the nails are generally due to an injury. When this is the case nothing can be done to remove the spot. It will grow out as the nails grow.

When the spots are found on several nails and are not due to injuries they are of nervous origin, and a good nerve tonic should be taken for a few weeks.

Nails, Ridges. Ridges on the nails are also due to impoverished health. They can be removed, if not too deep, by polishing the nails with a polishing paste.

Nails, the Growth of. The growth of the nails varies in different individuals. On young hands the growth is more rapid, and more so in summer than in winter. During the summer the growth of the nails is more marked in those on the right hand than on the left. This seems strange, but has been noted by more than one careful observer. The growth from the half-moon to the edge of the finger tip takes about four months.

<u>Neck, a Too-Thin.</u>
When the neck is too thin it
should be bathed with warm
water, dried, and thoroughly
massaged with a good cream
for feeding the tissues. This
should be done every night,
and a piece of cheesecloth
lightly wrapped around it to
keep the grease on the skin.

Health & Beauty Monthly

Epsom salt

Epsom salt is the common name for Magnesium sulfate
(or magnesium sulphate), a chemical compound
containing magnesium and sulfur hydrate. Epsom salt
has been traditionally used as a component of bath
salts and is used in flotation therapy where heavy
concentrations raise the bath water's specific gravity,
making the immersed body more buoyant.

Plenty of fattening foods should be taken, such as milk, eggs. A
glass of hot milk, slowly sipped, at bedtime will also help.

<u>Neck, Too Plump.</u> To reduce a too-plump neck, massage with a few
drops of a reducing lotion and practise neck-turning exercises, morning
and evening.

<u>Obesity.</u> Obesity can only be successfully treated by careful dieting and
reducing baths. Those who are inclined to put on weight should take advice
regarding their exercise and rest patterns. The chief meal of the day should
be the midday one, and it is best to take nothing solid after six in the
evening except a little fruit. Afternoon tea should consist of a cup of weak
tea and nothing to eat, unless it be a dry biscuit.

<u>Epsom Salts for Obesity.</u> For external use in obesity the Epsom salts
method is very efficacious. Take half a pound of Epsom salts and dissolve
it in a pint of soft hot water.

Into another pint of soft boiling water shave a tablet and a half of
white Castile soap. When the soap is dissolved, add the water to which the
Epsom salts was added and beat together very thoroughly. The mixture
should be massaged into the parts to be reduced every night and allowed to
remain on the skin till next morning.

This mixture is too drastic to use on the face but is excellent for the
hips, arms, and legs.

<u>Perfume.</u> What perfume shall be used must be left to individual choice. Some prefer a heavy Oriental scent, others the delicate fragrance of fresh flowers. In this matter it is best to study one's personality. The exotic-looking woman will be wise to choose some scent that will accord with her type, and young girls should decide on a flower scent which will suit their fresh youthfulness.

To perfume the hair sew a tiny sachet, perfumed with your favourite scent, into the lining of your hat, another in the corner of your shingle cap. This is better than spraying perfume on the hair, which often tends to encourage greyness. A few drops can also be added to the brilliantine you use for your hair or to the oil with which you massage the scalp.

<u>To perfume your dance frocks</u> spray a little perfume on the inner side of the hem of the skirt and on the inside of the bodice. Scent applied in this way gives a delightful perfume as the wearer dances, not too strong but very subtle.

A few drops put in the palm of the hand and the hands rubbed together is another way of applying scent that is very effective, and a few drops added to the water in which you clean your teeth will perfume the breath deliciously. But this should only be done on very special occasions.

To give a delightful suggestion of fresh violets, put a dessertspoonful of extract of violets into half a pint of tepid water. Dip a small sponge into this and sponge the body, allowing the liquid to dry on the skin. The scent will last for 24 hours when applied in this way, and any other perfume may be substituted for essence of violets if preferred.

To make delightful scent "cakes" for perfuming the wardrobe, millinery chest, etc., get ½ a lb. of lump paraffin and melt it. Stir into it 1 oz. of oil of verbena, 2 drachms

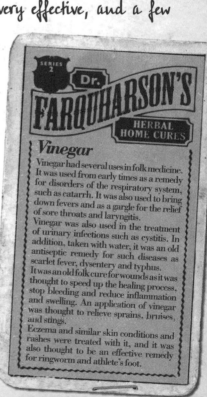

Series 2

DR. FARQUHARSON'S

HERBAL HOME CURES

Vinegar

Vinegar had several uses in folk medicine. It was used from early times as a remedy for disorders of the respiratory system, such as catarrh. It was also used to bring down fevers and as a gargle for the relief of sore throats and laryngitis.

Vinegar was also used in the treatment of urinary infections such as cystitis. In addition, taken with water, it was an old antiseptic remedy for such diseases as scarlet fever, dysentery and typhus.

It was an old folk cure for wounds as it was thought to speed up the healing process, stop bleeding and reduce inflammation and swelling. An application of vinegar was thought to relieve sprains, bruises, and stings.

Eczema and similar skin conditions and rashes were treated with it, and it was also thought to be an effective remedy for ringworm and athlete's foot.

of oil of cloves, and 2 drachms of oil of lavender. Stir well and pour the mixture into a shallow tin to harden. Cut into small rounds or squares and place in drawers and cupboards. It will give a delicious perfume. One of these cakes may be placed in the handbag to perfume the contents, if desired.

Perspiration, Excessive. The cause of excessive perspiration is generally very difficult to discover, but it is supposed to be of nervous origin. It may be general or only in the feet and hands or the arm-pits.

Sponging with equal parts of vinegar and water sometimes effects a cure, especially when followed by dusting with a powder composed of 5 oz. of powdered starch, 1 oz. of powdered alum, and 2 oz. of powdered orrisroot. The powders should be thoroughly mixed and passed through a fine sieve. When the perspiration is of nervous origin, a good tonic should be taken, and the amount of fruit and vegetables in the daily menu increased. A little watercress taken daily will be found very beneficial.

Pimples. Pimples are generally due to over-heated blood. Occasionally they are the result of poorness of blood, in which case there will be other signs of anaemia. When the latter is the cause, a tonic should be taken and plenty of nourishing foods. When due to overheated blood, all sweets and pastries should be avoided, and a dose of saline salts taken every morning. Plenty of water should be taken between meals, all the fresh fruit and vegetables possible, and as much exercise in the open as circumstances permit.

The following lotion may be dabbed on the pimples two or three times daily with a pad of cotton wool: 3 drachms of precipitated sulphur, 7 grains of powdered camphor, 15 grains of powdered tragacanth, 1½ oz. of lime water, 2 oz. of rosewater. Mix and apply to each individual pimple. Avoid the use of greasy creams while the pimples are noticeable.

Health & Beauty Monthly

UNDER-ARM DEODORANT
- A Rose Astringent Lotion

Bring to a boil 3 cups of white vinegar, remove to a bottle, and add
½ oz. Rosebuds
¼ oz. Myrtle berries
¼ oz. Camomile flowers
½ oz. Jamaica flowers.

Infuse the botanicals for 14 days and shake the bottle several times daily. Strain the solution carefully through fine cheesecloth and add an equal quantity of Rosewater.

<u>Potato, as a Bleach for the Skin.</u> The juice from a potato makes an excellent bleach for whitening the skin. Wash a large potato, cut it in slices, about ½ an inch thick, and rub over the face, neck, and hands.

Do it at night after thoroughly cleansing the skin, and allow the juice to remain on till next morning. Wash off with lukewarm water without soap.

Daphne PREFERS heR TaTTies mashed!

<u>Powder, how to Choose Complexion Powder.</u> When choosing powder remember that a fine sensitive skin requires a very fine powder, a coarse skin with enlarged pores a heavier make. Let the colour of your powder tone with that of your skin, and use a lighter powder for the neck and shoulders, when in evening dress, than for the face.

Powder should never be rubbed on the face. Apply it with little dabs, using a pad of cotton-wool.

Cotton-wool is more hygienic, as well as more effective, for applying powder. It can be used and thrown away, thus preventing any possibility of using a soiled puff to the face, which is very injurious to a clear, fresh complexion.

Complexion powder may now be obtained in flesh, naturelle, white, peach, ochre, and suntan, so there is no reason why each one should not obtain a powder in the shade which will be most becoming to her.

Many of the manufacturers of complexion powders are willing to supply samples in different shades so that a choice may be made of a really becoming shade before a box is purchased.

<u>Quince Seeds, a Beauty Lotion From.</u> A lotion for softening a very dry skin which has been made drier and harder by too much exposure to sun and wind can be made from quince seeds.

Take 2 drachms of quince seeds and add to them 2 drachms of pure glycerine and 8 oz. of extract of witch-hazel. Allow to stand for twelve hours, shaking the mixture from time to time. Strain off. Dissolve

5 grains of borax in a little warm water and add to the lotion, and add gradually, shaking occasionally, ½ oz. of surgical spirit.

The lotion should be applied with a pad of cotton-wool.

Recipes for Improving the Skin.—Orange Skin Food. Take 4 drachms of white wax and 2 drachms of spermaceti. Put them in an earthenware jar and stand the jar in hot water. When melted add 2 oz. of oil of sweet almonds, 2 drachms of orange-flower water, and ½ a drachm of oil of orange. Beat together and put into pomade pots. To be massaged into the skin.

Benzoin Skin Food. Take 1 oz. of lanolin, ½ an oz. of cocoa butter, ½ an oz. of spermaceti, and melt together in an earthenware jar. Add 3 oz. of oil of almonds and beat together, adding, while beating, 60 drops of simple tincture of benzoin. This cream is a trifle hard until it comes into contact with the skin, when it immediately melts and becomes soft and easily massaged into the pores.

Rest. Rest as you go, should be the motto of every woman who wishes to remain youthful. Half an hour's rest in the afternoon is an excellent plan for those who can manage it, but if that is not possible, and to the business woman it is quite out of the question, a little rest should be taken early in the evening.

If every business woman on returning home in the evening would, after removing her outdoor things, stretch herself out flat, without a pillow, on the floor or a hard couch, and try and make her mind a blank, closing the eyes, she would find that she would be more rested than after two or three hours' sleep.

The room should be darkened, for it is practically impossible to rest thoroughly in a brightly-lit room, and, if the eyes have been used all day, two pieces of cotton-wool moistened with boric lotion should be laid over the closed eyes.

<u>Reducing Corsets.</u> For reducing purposes the rubber corset has had a great vogue. It should be worn night and day over a thin vest and a reducing bath taken every two days.

The corset or belt should be obtained in the correct measurements, that is, the size of the hips or waist at the time of starting wearing it. If too small the rubber will tear or split, the corset or belt being rendered useless.

<u>Shoes.</u>—<u>To beautify the Feet.</u> The woman with small, dainty feet, slim ankles, and a good instep, can wear almost any type of shoe and yet know that her feet will be admired. But the one with a large foot, especially if it be broad as well as long, must choose her footgear with great care.

A laced—up shoe is not for her. A single strap across the instep will help to reduce the apparent size for street wear, and in the evening she can wear shoes of a more ornamental type. If her foot is very long but narrow, she should wear pointed toes, but the large, broad foot should adopt the French style of shoe, with a short round toe. The heels should be high for evening and home wear.

Dark leather and black satin shoes should be worn on every possible occasion, and the dull tones of hose for daylight. Gold shoes tend to make the feet appear smaller, but silver tinsel should be avoided.

<u>Shoulders, to Correct Round.</u> To correct round shoulders, or a slight stoop, practise the following exercises morning and evening and at any other time when a few spare minutes are available:

1st Exercise. Stand erect, facing a door or wall, with the feet about 12 in. from the door. Head up and shoulders held well back. Stretch the arms out, on a level with the shoulders, and place the hands with the palms against the door. Press the body forwards towards the door, resisting the pressure with the arms till the head is close to the door. Rest and repeat.

2nd Exercise. Sit on the floor with the feet stretched out straight in front, knees rigid. Raise the arms to the level of the shoulders, bend them at the elbows and place the hands with the fingers touching beneath the chin.

Part the fingers gradually, pressing the elbows back as far as possible. Rest and repeat. When practising these two exercises the shoulder blades will be pressed backwards and the back strengthened.

Lying flat on the floor with a hard pillow beneath the shoulders, but not under the head, is also excellent for correcting round shoulders or a too-pronounced curve at the back of the waist.

<u>Shoulders, to Whiten.</u> To whiten the shoulders put 1 oz. of white wax and ½ an oz. of spermaceti in an earthenware jar. Stand the jar in a pan of hot water till both have melted. Add 2 oz. of olive oil and stir. When mixed, add ½ a teaspoonful of powdered borax and beat, adding, while beating, 25 drops of simple tincture of benzoin.

Bathe the shoulders with soft, lukewarm water, dry, and massage some of the mixture well into them.

<u>Shoulders, to Whiten for an Evening.</u> To whiten the shoulders temporarily, bathe with warm milk, sprinkle thickly with fine oatmeal, and rub the oatmeal into the skin until it is quite dry. Then add the usual complexion powder.

<u>Sleep.</u> The amount of sleep required by the average adult varies from seven to nine hours. Very nervy people should get as much rest and sleep as possible, and the growing girl cannot have too much. The busy woman should try and secure eight hours, if not every night at least four or five times a week, for sleep is "Nature's sweet restorer", and is a wonderful recipe for smoothing lines and wrinkles and giving a sparkle to the eyes.

Never sleep in a badly ventilated room. Whatever the weather, have the top of the window open at least a foot. Let

the bedclothes be warm but light, and see that the room is thoroughly darkened. It is most injurious to the eyes to wake in a bright light, and will cause fine lines and wrinkles around them.

The deep, frowning wrinkles which are so unbecoming can often be traced to no other cause than waking in a bright light. It does not really matter whether one goes to bed at eleven or two in the morning, provided that the hours allotted to sleep can be taken consecutively. The old idea that sleep obtained before midnight was more beneficial is quite an exploded one. It is having the amount of rest and sleep that matters, not at what time it is taken.

See that you get your eight, or more, hours every night, but do not worry at what time you get them. If you are inclined to sleeplessness try and go to bed at the same hour each night, so that sleeping at that time may become a habit. It is a great help in cases of insomnia.

<u>Styes.</u> Styes are little swellings on the eyelids which are in reality a kind of small boil. They are very painful and unsightly, and generally a sign of poor health, especially when several appear one after the other.

Occasionally the stye may be due to eye strain, but this is a very rare cause. In some cases a stye can be cured by pulling out the nearest eyelash, in others small poultices are the best treatment. When a succession of styes occur a tonic should be taken, such as iron or hypophosphites.

<u>Sun-Baths.</u> The first sun-bath should be taken with great caution. Remember that the head and back of the neck must never be exposed to the fierce rays of the sun.

The first sun-bath should never exceed ten minutes, and the feet alone should be

SERIES 2

Dr.

FARQUHARSON'S

HERBAL HOME CURES

Sunstroke

An old method of preventing sunstroke was to wear a cabbage leaf inside the crown of a hat.

If someone was suffering from bad sunstroke it was recommended that the person's clothing should be loosened and cold water poured over him or her.

Alternatively, clothing was to be removed and the patient covered with a sheet that had to be kept drenched with cold water.

Another cure involved the application of mustard leaves to the nape of the neck of the person suffering from sunstroke.

exposed on the first occasion. Two or three days should be devoted to sun-bathing the feet alone, next the legs may be exposed to the sun, later the arms, and finally the back and upper part of the body, increasing the time as one grows accustomed to the baths.

SERIES 2

Dr.

FARQUHARSON'S

HERBAL HOME CURES

Sunburn

A cut strawberry rubbed on an area of sunburn was thought to bring relief. Grated potato mixed with olive oil was also thought to relieve sunburn. Vinegar rubbed on the skin was used to treat sunburn.

Cucumber juice was used to cool sunburn, and it was sometimes mixed with rose water. Crushed marigolds were used to ease sunburn, as was glycerine, sometimes mixed with rose water. Washing the sunburn in sage tea was another suggested remedy.

Egg white applied to the skin in layers with time being allowed for each layer to dry before the other layer was applied was considered to soothe sunburn. Buttermilk was also supposed to ease the pain of sunburn.

An old cure for sunburn involved mixing cream, lemon, brandy, alum and sugar. This was boiled, skimmed, cooled and applied to the skin.

Another old cure was based on grapes. A bunch of green grapes was sprinkled with a mixture of salt and powdered alum. The grapes were wrapped in paper and baked. The juice was squeezed out of the grapes and was then applied to the area of skin suffering from sunburn.

<u>Sunburn.</u> Sunburn is of two kinds, the deep tan shade which is often very attractive looking, and the less becoming, but more easily removed, red type.

The very fair, fine skins are those which, in the majority of cases, burn red, and these should be protected, when exposed to the sun during the hotter hours of the day, by applying a little pure olive oil beneath whatever vanishing cream and complexion powder is used.

To remove red sunburn, bathe the skin with lukewarm milk and apply a little cold cream. Never use a bleach to a skin that has burnt red.

<u>To remove Tan.</u> Soap and water should not be applied to a badly tanned face. Cleanse it with lukewarm milk and water and a paste of fine oatmeal. To remove the tan, dab the following lotion over the skin with a pad of cotton-wool every night after cleansing the face as advised above.

To make the lotion, dissolve 2 drachms of powdered borax in half a pint of distilled water. Add the strained juice of a lemon and shake thoroughly. Apply as directed above.

To prevent tan and the dark shades of sunburn apply a little calamine lotion to the face before dusting with the complexion powder generally used. Those who freckle and tan easily should use an ochre shade of powder when at the sea or in the country. This shade of powder offers a greater resistance to the rays of the sun than any other.

Teeth. The shape of the teeth and the way they are set in the mouth cannot be altered once adult age has been reached, but clean, white, well-kept teeth are within the reach of every woman who will devote a little time to their care. Regular cleaning, night and morning, using a tooth paste at night and a dentifrice in the morning, will keep them clean, and a rub with a small piece of perfectly clean chamois leather will make them glisten like the pearls to which beautiful teeth are so often compared. The water used for cleaning the teeth should be lukewarm and the brush chosen firm without being too hard. A hard brush will irritate the gums, and unless the gums are healthy the teeth cannot be kept in good condition.

When cleansing the teeth do not neglect the back ones because they are not visible to the eye. Those are the teeth that do the work of masticating the food, and unless they are thoroughly cleansed every night particles of food will lodge in the crevices and set up decay during the hours of sleep. The teeth should be cleansed morning and night, but if one cleansing must be missed it is better, for the teeth, that it should be the morning.

Tartar is the great enemy to healthy teeth, and as soon as any is noticed it should be removed. In the early stages a little powdered

Toothache

IN FOLKLORE, prevention was better than cure. Several charms were suggested to ward off toothache. One rather macabre charm against toothache was a tooth taken from a corpse and worn round the neck. A double nut carried in the pocket was also supposed to keep toothache at bay. An ancient Egyptian cure that involved applying the body of a freshly killed mouse to the aching tooth.

A Welsh cure involved pounding lizards and fern beetles in an iron pot and making a powder from them. The wet forefinger was then dipped in the powder and applied to the tooth frequently until the tooth supposedly painlessly came out.

Another remedy involved the person suffering from toothache lying on the opposite side of the body from the side where the toothache was. Three drops of rue juice were then dropped into the ear on the same side as the aching tooth. It was allowed to remain for an hour or two, after which the toothache was supposed to have disappeared.

Bandage

Whisky was involved too. A piece of cotton wadding or cotton wool moistened with whisky was placed on the tooth. In another, a small piece of strong brown paper was dipped in whisky, sprinkled with pepper and applied to the face at the point where the aching tooth was. This was covered with a flannel bandage and left until a cure was effected. A piece of cloth dipped in a mixture of creosote, brandy and sweet spirits of nitre was held to be curative. Alternatively, a little bryonia liniment was added to warm water. This mixture was added to a glass of warm water and held in the mouth over the tooth that was giving problems.

Fresh ginger was chewed to dull the pain of toothache. Ginger was also used as an internal cure. Ground ginger was mixed with Epsom salts and added to hot water.

Cinnamon oil applied directly to the tooth was thought to bring relief to toothache while a piece of cotton-wool soaked in oil of cloves applied in the same way was a common popular cure. Peppermint oil was also used to ease toothache. Onion juice was also put on cotton-wool and applied to the aching tooth, as was the juice of fresh parsley.

magnesia on a moistened tooth brush will remove it, but if it is of long standing the services of a dentist must be enlisted to have the matter dealt with.

To whiten discoloured teeth, mix together ½ oz. of the finest powdered pumice stone and 1 oz. of precipitated chalk. Use this mixture once a month, not oftener, until the colour of the teeth has improved. An inexpensive dentifrice can be made at home by mixing 2 oz. of spirit of wine with 1 oz. of essence of violets and ½ a drachm of spirits of peppermint. Shake thoroughly and keep tightly corked. A few drops should be added to the water in which the teeth are cleaned.

A visit to the dentist should be paid every six months. If there is any damage to a tooth the matter can be put right at once, and so save further trouble. When a tooth has started to decay the decay spreads very rapidly, and often serious damage is done before it begins to ache.

Tooth Brushes. A small tooth brush is to be preferred to a large one. It will pass round the mouth more easily and can be used to clean the back teeth in a more satisfactory manner.

The brush should not be too hard and it is a good plan to keep two, using them on alternate days. Brushes should be kept where a current of air can pass over them. It is best to hang them up, and every other day they should be dipped in a mixture of peroxide and lukewarm water, a teaspoonful of peroxide of hydrogen (10 vol.) to half a tumbler of water.

To prevent Decay. To prevent the teeth from decaying, add 3 or 4 drops of myrrh to the water in which the teeth are cleaned. Once or twice a week is often enough for this.

Throat, to Whiten for an Evening. Wash in warm milk and water, dry, and rub over with a little rosewater and glycerine. While the skin is still damp dust thickly with complexion powder, white if possible. After ten minutes take a piece of chamois leather, or a soft towel, and rub gently.

The surplus powder will be rubbed off, and the skin will remain white and smooth. This method can also be used for the arms and is to be preferred to liquid powder as it will not rub off on the dress or the partner's coat sleeves when dancing.

Throat, to Whiten the. To whiten the throat take the whites only of 3 eggs and beat them up stiffly with 3 oz. of oil of sweet almonds and 1 oz. of honey.

Bathe the throat with warm water, and, after drying the skin, spread the mixture over it. Do not rub it in, merely spread it on rather thickly and leave till next morning. Wash off with oatmeal and lukewarm water.

Tomatoes. Tomato juice makes an excellent bleach for the skin. Cut the tomato in half and rub the pulp over the face, throat, arms, and

Throats, sore

THERE WERE several old cures for sore throats. Some of these were stranger than others.

In one rather weird cure a piece of raw bacon was tied to a length of strong cotton. The person suffering from the sore throat had to swallow the bacon while holding tightly to the cotton. The fat was then pulled back up by the cotton and this exercise was repeated half a dozen times. A black cashmere stocking that had been worn for a week then had the sole of it sprinkled with eucalyptus. This was placed against the throat and the rest of the stocking wrapped around the neck and pinned. The patient then retired for the night.

Old cure

Another old cure involved filling a stocking or large sock with cooking salt, which was sometimes heated first. The sock or stocking was wound round the neck of the person with the sore throat before he or she retired for the night.

There were several other more ordinary-sounding cures. Some camphor was added to a wineglass of brandy. This mixture was poured over a lump of loaf sugar. The sugar lump was allowed to dissolve in the mouth of the person who was suffering from the sore throat. This was repeated every hour until four doses had been taken. After this the sore throat was confidently predicted to have disappeared.

An infusion of elderberries sweetened with honey sipped slowly was a suggested remedy. An infusion of yarrow root taken three times a day was also supposed to bring relief. Eating onions boiled in molasses was supposed to be particularly effective if the sore throat was accompanied by hoarseness.

A weak solution of salt was used as a gargle to bring relief to sore throats, as were a mixture of lemon juice and warm water, and a dilute mixture of iodine and water. A little vinegar added to water was also used as a gargle, as was an infusion of mustard.

An infusion of sage leaves with added vinegar and a little honey was used as a gargle. Other gargles included barley water, sage tea, borage tea, dock, peppermint, eucalyptus oil, witch hazel and myrrh. Hot vinegar was used as an inhalation.

Garlic juice taken internally was thought to help. Eating leeks was also used as a remedy, as was eating onions. A hot tea made from rosemary was also used in the treatment of sore throats, and comfrey was a popular remedy taken internally. A hot infusion of yarrow was also taken for the relief of sore throats.

hands. Leave it on for about an hour, then wash off with rosewater to which a few drops of simple tincture of benzoin have been added. When mixing rosewater and benzoin the proportions should be 10 drops of the benzoin to 1 oz of rosewater. Always use the double distilled rosewater.

Waist, to Reduce the. A slim, supple waist is essential to modern fashions. Those who are stiff and feel that the waist muscles are not as supple as they might be should practise the following exercises every night and morning. Night is an excellent time for exercising. It relaxes the muscles and often helps to woo sleep for the sleepless.

1st Exercise. Stand erect, feet together, shoulders back, eyes looking level, and the knees rigid. Place the hands on the hips and twist the upper part of the body to the right as far as it will go. Swing it back slowly and swing round to the left. Rest and repeat. Do this from ten to twenty times.

2nd Exercise. Bend the arms and crouch down on the floor with the knees bent till nearly sitting on the floor. Strike upwards, straightening the knees and raising the arms at the same time, trying to reach as high as possible and springing to the toes. Count one, two, three, and repeat.

Walk.—A Graceful Walk. For a graceful walk the figure should be held easily, the shoulders drawn back, and the chest held forward. The head should be held high, with the chin slightly tilted. The knees should be straight and the toes slightly turned out. The average woman turns out her toes too much, and consequently the feet appear to be sprawling.

To be correct the feet should have an angle of 45°, and the knees also should be turned slightly outwards. The knee, when bent, should be vertically in a line with the toe. When advancing the foot, keep the knee straight and let the length of your step be such as will suit your height. A small figure taking very long strides is far from graceful.

As each step is made, the toes and ball of the foot should reach the ground first, the heel following immediately. When the sole of the foot is placed down first it gives a heavy awkward gait.

To give height to a small figure the knees should be kept straight. Allowing the knees to sag, "cab horse knees" as they are often called, will

Daphne's Saturday Beauty Regime

(Fae Maw's Mither's Health and Beauty Book)

6.00am — Get up. Drink water fresh from the tap, with juice of a squeezed lemon. Remove adhesive plaster from between the eyes, and inspect for any improvement in frown lines.
Note to self: Try not to laugh today, for fear of making wrinkle lines and crows-feet worse.

6.10am — Bathe eyelids in cold water to help soreness. Cut two chunks of cucumber and rub on closed eyelids, to relieve tiredness.
Drink a quart of saline salts – prevention for acne. Make quick facepack paste with oatmeal and water and place on skin. Take teaspoon of olive oil with teaspoon of grape juice for sallow skin and swallow.

6.15am — While waiting for face pack to work: do exercises for ankles – to reduce – sit on a low chair and extend leg and rotate foot. Then the other one.

6.20am — Standing behind chair, hands on chair, do Russian ballet dancer's bending exercises. Wash off face pack.

6.25am — Stand in front of open window (in dressing gown!) and do big breathing exercises.

6.30am — Whiten the arms – and improve pointed elbows by rubbing them with fine oatmeal. Rub elbows with lemons to whiten them, then rub upper arms. Do massage for 'too plump arms' – use camphor and orange flower water and massage well.

6.45am	Soak cotton wool in turpentine and bind over corn on inside of little toe.
6.50am	Lie on kitchen table, no pillow, for bad back for half an hour until Maw gets up and lays it for breakfast; if Hen is not there first. Note to self: if Hen is on the table, get up earlier tomorrow.
7.10am	Eat two raw carrots for complexion, and one apple for the skin. Eat one tomato to whiten the eyes. Eat four lettuce leaves, no oil, or salad cream, (unless really desperate, and if the Twins are up and make jokes about rabbits) and three watercress leaves. One radish.
7.15am	For breakfast, one pint of milk but only if on 'milk and potato' diet. If on new Hollywood Diet, eat a grapefruit. If not, a fry up.
7.20/ 7.45am	(depending on which diet) Brisk walk for the constitution.
8.00am	Help Maw with breakfast things.
9.00am	If no one in kitchen, start perfume scent cakes for perfuming the wardrobe. Verbena, cloves, lavender – cook up, and cut into cakes when set. Also make massage cream, and follow instructions for Maw's Mither's moisturising cream with one pound of lard and a bottle of rosewater. Boil up lard, with rosewater. Once it's cooled, put the cream into jars. Braw!
10.00am	Make butter muslin pouches to use in bath as a calming skin tonic.
11.30am	Snack: fruit – raspberries and watercress if on new Hollywood Diet. If not on diet, fruit scone with raspberry jam, and a pancake, and a couple of sausage rolls for energy.

8.00pm	Put glycerine on lips, and practice saying 'prunes' and 'prisms' 50 times to tighten up lips and look young. Whistle 'The Lone Ranger' three times, to tighten the lip muscles, as per Maw's Mither's instructions. (note, Maw's Mither did not specify which tune. Maybe some nineteenth century music hall epic would be better?)
8.15pm	Take nerve tonic, just in case I get anxious in the future.
8.20pm	Free time.
10.00pm	Run bath for the 'too stout'. Dissolve 2 – 4oz Epsom Salts into bath water. Add bran and lemon pack in butter muslin pouch. Head for bed, but only after –
10.30pm	Make camomile tea, with sugar, for complexion. Eat an apple – also for the complexion. Maybe eat meringues with the apple, if there are any left, and add a little double cream to the meringues to reward self for long day at beauty improvements. If there is any single cream, maybe pour that over double cream and meringues as it tastes better and Maw's Mither's book says cream and butter is very good for the beauty in general.
10.40pm	Rub sweet almond oil into the eyelids. Massage forehead with cold cream in smooth strokes. If feeling like a cold is coming, or a bit chesty, lay a cabbage leaf across the chest (might need to lie down to keep cabbage leaf in place, so do this last thing). Cover face with lardy/rosewater cream and then wipe off with butter muslin. Paint bunion with tincture of iodine. Practice neck-turning exercises and put on neck-reducing lotion.
10.55pm	Take Epsom salts and soap mixture, as made earlier, and massage into any bits that need reducing.

Might take longer than ten minutes though. Could always do it in the morning instead. If time, check store cupboard for any last minute things to eat that might go off before morning, and eat them to ensure no hunger pangs in night, which might cause insomnia. Maw's Mithen's book says drink cold milk to ensure good sleep, and I'm sure she'd not mind me having a wee slice of fruit cake with it to settle the tummy before bed.

11.10pm	Cut a potato, and after cleansing the face, and using an astringent, rub the potato all over the face. Allow the juice to remain on the skin overnight. Maybe fry up potatoes, just to make sure there is no waste, and eat with salt and vinegar.
11.20pm	Do shoulder exercises last thing.
11.25pm	Clean teeth, and use chamois to polish the teeth, and make them glisten like pearls. Do not neglect the back ones for overall beauty.
11.30pm	A final glass of lime water to keep warts at bay. Put on gloves with holes cut in them for ventilation, and fill with Daphne's home made handcream. Place cabbage leaves on chest, if Maw can spare more than one. Braw!
11.35pm	Get into bed – try to get seven hours sleep. Do not put in curlers.
11.36pm	Set alarm for 6.00am
00.30am	If unable to sleep, wake Maw, make tea and blether.

lose a couple of inches from the apparent height besides giving a loose, floppy look which destroys dignity and grace. Sitting and rising from a chair is another test of easy graceful movements. When rising let your feet rest firmly on the ground and, with one movement from the hips, rise, moving forwards at the same time.

Warts. To cure a wart or a succession of warts try taking a wineglassful of lime water every day. Any chemist will supply the lime water, and it is one of the simplest and best remedies, far superior to interfering with the wart externally, which often leaves a bad scar.

Warts, when they appear in succession, are a sign of insufficient lime in the blood. The lime water may be taken in a little milk, but it is best to take it alone.

Water.—A Beautifier. Water is a tissue builder, and the woman who wishes to keep her skin firm and youthful should drink at least a quart of tap water daily. The water should be taken, a ½ pint at a time, between, not with, meals.

Water, Home—Made Lavender. To make lavender water at home take 12 oz. of surgical spirit and add to it 1 drachm of oil of lavender, 10 drops of essence of rose, 20 drops of essence of bergamot, and 1 drachm of essence of musk. Shake together till thoroughly blended and cork the bottle tightly. A few drops added to the washing water will give it a delightful perfume.

WARTS

ONION JUICE was suggested as a cure for warts, as were dandelion juice, leek juice, mullein juice, rue juice and the juice of St John's wort. An infusion of marigold, or the crushed fresh flowers of marigold, was used also as a remedy, and the warts were also rubbed night and morning with cinnamon oil in an attempt to get rid of them

Another recommended remedy was the rubbing of the warts with a raw potato, and yet another involved rubbing the warts with castor oil.

Thyme juice boiled with pepper in wine and the juice of teasel roots boiled in wine were both regarded as remedies. The juice of wheat ears was mixed with salt to form another cure for warts, and willow bark was burnt and its ashes mixed with vinegar to be applied as lotion to the warts.

A more curious cure involved tying a horse hair round the individual warts and applying spider webs, pig's blood or the juice from ants. Rubbing the wart with the blood of eels was another suggested old remedy.

Several supposed remedies involved burying whatever the wart was rubbed with, in the belief that as the buried object rotted away the wart would disappear. In one of these the wart was cut open and rubbed with a sour apple that was afterwards buried. In another, a piece of meat was rubbed on the wart and buried, a stipulation being that the meat had to be stolen. Alternatively, the stolen meat could be thrown away instead of being buried when it had been rubbed on the wart.

Raw bacon was something else that could be rubbed on the wart and buried. The inside of a broad bean could also be used in this way.

Weather, Beauty in Foggy. A few days of foggy weather can be very disastrous to both hair and complexion. After being out in the fog give the eyes a warm boric bath, and if they feel very dull and are smarting, which is often the case, dip two pieces of cotton-wool in cold, weak tea and place them over the closed eyes.

Wipe the face over with a soft towel and massage into the skin some good cold cream. Wipe off and apply some vanishing cream and fresh powder. This makes the face feel fresher and removes all the grime left by the fog. Give the hair a good brushing, especially if it is fair or auburn. Damp slightly by rubbing over with a moist towel and re-set the waves.

Fog always takes the wave out of the hair unless it, fortunately, happens to be a natural one, and even then there is the chance that it will appear damp and straggling for a few hours after being exposed to a foggy atmosphere.

Give the hair a shampoo as soon as the foggy spell is over, for that is the only way that it can really be made bright and fluffy again.

Weather, Beauty in Hot. During a very hot spell the woman whose skin is abnormally greasy should use an astringent lotion as a foundation for her powder in place of vanishing cream. The lotion will prevent the skin from "giving" and the powder will remain on longer. Women with this type of skin should use a heavy make of powder, those with a fine skin a lighter.

Liquid powder does not allow the skin to "give" as much as the dry kind, and for that reason is frequently used during the hotter months of the year, especially by women with a greasy skin. After the powder has been applied, any which has settled around the nostrils, or in any lines or wrinkles, should be lightly wiped off. To allow it to remain not only makes the wrinkles more noticeable than they otherwise would be, but helps to deepen them permanently.

A little of the liquid powder rubbed over moist hands will keep them cool and improve their appearance, and those who walk much in warm weather will find that talcum powder dusted into the soles of the stockings and the insides of the shoes will help to prevent the feet from feeling hot and tired.

Give the hair plenty of combing and an air bath whenever possible. Exposure to the rays of the sun during the hotter hours of the day is not good for the hair, but ventilation will improve the colour, making it brighter and glossier, and help to increase the growth.

Weight. The question of the correct weight for different heights is one that has varied a great deal of late years. The "fine" woman with her large hips and over-developed bust is no longer the type that is admired.

Instead we cultivate the slim, graceful figure, and slimming has taken the place of "filling out" the figure which was the fashion in Victorian days. Weight even in these days varies with age, the older one grows the heavier one gets. The exception to this is the growing girl, who often puts on weight between sixteen and twenty and loses it after that.

After thirty both men and women gradually increase in weight unless special dieting is resorted to.

Wrinkles. Wrinkles are due to the shrinking of the fatty tissues beneath the skin. As the tissues shrink and shrivel up, the skin covering them falls into little lines and wrinkles, more or less deep, according to the amount of fatty tissue which has shrunk and the type of skin. Some skins are naturally more elastic than others.

Generally the wrinkles which form at the sides of the mouth, running from nose to mouth, are the deepest, for it is on the cheeks that there is generally the greatest loss of fatty tissue. In early youth the cheeks are full and round and the skin over them taut, but as the years pass the tissues deteriorate, the cheeks become either hollow or flabby, and deep lines form.

"Oh dear". Wrinkles!

Only by stimulating the muscles can these wrinkles be smoothed out. Skin foods alone are useless. They may feed the skin, but as long as the muscles remain flabby the cheeks cannot regain the rounded contour of youth. To treat the epidermis or outer skin is useless — one must go deeper to secure results. One must attack the muscles and conquer their relaxed and flabby condition and the rest is easy, the wrinkles will fade away.

The fine little wrinkles which form around the eyes and beneath them are often the result of a too-dry skin. Very dry skin always wrinkles early in life, and it should never be washed in hot water, or soap used to the face, and, even more important, when water is used the skin should be thoroughly dried and dusted with a good dusting, not a complexion, powder. Cold water is excellent for preventing wrinkles, whether the skin is dry or naturally greasy, but it must be soft cold water and the skin be thoroughly dried, for nothing is more productive of wrinkles than to allow water to dry on the skin.

To stimulate the muscles a really strong astringent lotion should be used, and when possible electrical treatment given at least twice a week. When this is not possible, massage should take its place, and it is best to use a "patter", working upwards with firm, hard pats.

Do not fear making the skin red; when it becomes red it is a good sign—it proves that the circulation of the blood is being increased, and this will help in removing the wrinkles and improving the skin generally.

Dear Margaret,

I was looking back at some of your letters. I do understand — all these years. I was having a smile — everything has worked out so well, but, my, you do have your hands full!

I hope you will remember that little book I gave you all these years ago. Do you still have it? Perhaps Daphne and Maggie will learn something from it? I do hope so.

Thankyou for your latest news and snaps. I have them by me as I write.

Hen is getting so tall now, and Joe is so grown-up. Quite the young man! How do you all fit into that flat?

Your little cottage sounds delightful, great fun!

Your loving Mother.

She's right! Maggie and Daphne both love this old notebook! And little does Mither know that I know most o' these off by heart — every word.
I can remember the day I got it — and that wisnae the day nor yesterday —and I can tell you without a word o' a lie — Mithers know a thing or two!

Maw Broon

102

BOLD, READY, ABLE & WILLING

GLEBE STREET SCHOOL
FRIENDS OF THE SCHOOL ASSOCIATION
The Glebe Street School Library Fund Appeal
"STAIN REMOVAL, HANDY HINTS & SUCHLIKE"

This wee pamphlet came about because of our afternoon teas, which are usually here at Number 10. Some of the ladies say it's easier for me to have them round here, what wi' me having the Bairn and the Twins tae look after, and we've got the big table and enough chairs, but I know it's because my tea and my cakes and fruit scones are the best! That's why they like to come here - and they don't have to do the washing-up either ! There was quite a gathering that particular afternoon - Mrs Gow of course, Mrs McSwell, Mrs McSpey (who reads the tea-leaves), Mrs Murphy from 25 Elm Street, Mrs McNab, Mrs Jones, Jessie from over the back wall, Bella Mackay from across the road, and Aggie and Nellie Pry.

They were all talking at once and then Mrs Murphy got up to go somewhere, and tripped on the rug but stopped herself falling by grabbing on to Jessie who grabbed the tablecloth - Well - the teapot went ower with an awfy crash- most of the cups and saucers as well - and the jam - the butter- all ower my best tablecloth !

My good china wasn't broken but there were stains everywhere - and of course all the ladies started fussin' about cleanin' up the mess. Then it started .... "I ken the best way o' getting rid o' tea stains - "and then the rest all chimed in and started arguing... about the tea stains, the grease marks - Jings! It was a right hullaballoo !

They settled down eventually, and we made more tea, and got to talking about all these handy hints and wee tips. Turns out that the Broons' remedies for most things work the best, though there's some good yins fae the ladies too.

Anyway - we decided to write some of them down, because Aggie and Nelly Pry are always lookin' for ways of raisin' money - This time for The Glebe Street School Library Fund Appeal, so, we thought we could let them use oor secrets, and we can pass on some of our wee wisdoms. So - Mrs Murphy offered to type it all out, and she managed most of it before she had that bad fall in the street, she'll get round to the rest one day. Anyway, we hope you find something here to help you !

Maw Broon & Ladies who 'Afternoon Tea' at 10 Glebe Street.

The Afternoon Tea Ladies at Number 10 Glebe Street

About The Remedies

We've all got our own wee store of household hints - those wee tips about this an' that. Some of these hints help us be thrifty about the cookin', and some are easier ways of carrying out everyday tasks and minimising the drudgery that is part an' parcel of runnin' a busy hoose. There's eleven o' us Broons, and I don't know which o' them cause mair trouble - the auld yins or the Twins and the Bairn. They dinnae mean ony hairm maist o' the time.Some handy hints save us time though and some, of course increase efficiency, which me as a modern Maw, has read a' aboot in a' the magazines that I read at the Doctor's and the Dentist's.

Special Hints

We've all got special hints to improve the food that we serve up for tea, and hints which just mean that nothing is allowed to go to waste. We all have special secrets about things like, the polishing of furniture, the cleaning of Paw's chair, the laundering of clothes, gettin' rid of stains. Some of these hints have been passed down to us from my own Maw and Paw's Maw; some we have learned from our own experience, or bletherin' over the back green wall. That Mrs Gow kens a'thing she says - Aye that'll be right !

Of course, there's lots that everyone knows - like, that you must wash your knife and hands in cold water, not hot, after cutting onions to get rid of the smell and everybody in oor hoose knows that sausages should be pricked with a fork before being cooked in order to stop them bursting.

Most folk readin' this then, will know many of the hints - but if there's just one wee tip that helps you save that treasured rug or bit o' furniture, or saves you slavin' for hours over something, then this wee book is all worthwhile. A lot of remedies are common sense, and we all agree that sometimes the best remedy to a problem is to sit and have a cup of tea and a wee think, so this book starts with exactly that - all about tea and how to make a great cup. Then we've sorted all the things into alphabetical order tae make it easier.

To Make a nice Pot of Tea

Fill your best china teapot with boiling water and let it stand until it is heated through - This is called warmin' the pot. Then pour the water out. For each cup of tea measure into the pot ½ to 1 teaspoon of tea, and a cup of fresh boiling water. You'll get to know the right balance after a while - it depends on what kind of tea you like, and the quality of it. Let it stand with the teapot lid on, covered with a tea cosy, for 3 minutes. You'll need a tea strainer that sits over the cup. Pour your tea !

If you like a wee drop milk, Paw's Maw always used to say 'put a wee drap o' milk in first, so your tea doesn't spoil your good china'.

Beer Stains

Fresh beer stains will come oot nae bother in a normal wash these days wi' a biological powder. Beer spilt on yer guid cairpets will no' leave a stain if the spill is dealt with right away. Sook up as much of the spill using absorbent cloths or kitchen roll, then awfy gently work on the mark wi' warm water and a wee dab o' detergent.

Clothes marked with dried-in beer stains'll need tae be soaked for a wee while in a bucket wi' warm water and detergent before washing. Some o' yon darker beers - like Broon Ale can be a wee problem tae shift'; Try rubbing a wee bit glycerine into the stain to loosen it off, and leave it for a while before soaking the article in warm water and borax. Then rinse well and wash as normal with a biological powder.

Beetroot Stains

We're a' great beetroot fans - it's awfy guid for ye, though it has a wee effect on the colour o' your whatisnames down below, an' it can make a demon o' a stain if you drop it. But don't despair! With oor lot, best serve up the beetroot sliced - no' in wee balls - as the next thing you know, they're rollin' aboot the tablecloth like a blow-fitba' game!

If the stain is fresh, dab on a paste made with detergent and lukewarm water. Work it gently through the stain, then plunge the garment in warm water and leave it for half an hour or so to loosen the stain before rinsing it oot. Or, dab some lemon juice onto the stain and leave it on for a while, in the sunlight, before washing it. If this disnae work and the fabric is white cotton or linen, you can try soaking it in a household bleach solution, BUT READ THE INSTRUCTIONS ON THE BOTTLE. Rinse well before washing.

Blood

Blood is quite easy to get off most fabrics if the stain is fresh. Maggie went through that awfy phase o' havin' nosebleeds at the drap o' a hat.

Soaking the fabric in cold, salty water might well be all that is needed to remove the mark, but the older the stain, the longer it will have to be soaked, and this is no' advisable for woollen fabrics.

If the bloodstain is old, mix up one part glycerine to two parts lukewarm water and dab it on the fabric to help to loosen it ; this avoids the need for such a lengthy soak. A wee soak in a solution of biological washing powder and water or two tablespoons of borax in a litre of water can also help before the garment is washed.

Non-washable articles clothing that have been stained with blood can be sponged with cold salty water, but add a wee drop ammonia.

On carpets, a pinch o' salt sprinkled onto wet bloodstains will absorb most of the blood. The area then needs to be gently rubbed with cold, salty water. Remember to work from the outside of the stain in the way.

Another way is to rub a paste of cornflour and water gently into the stain. When this has dried, brush off the cornflour and repeat 'till you're done.

Candle Wax

When there's an 'auld yin' in the faimily, that's as auld as oor auld yin.... there's a tempation to cover an entire cake wi' candles, and attempt to light the lot - but by the time you get number eighty-something lit, number 1 has all but expired and dripped its wax doon the cake and onto the cloth ! Then when the auld fella tries tae blaw them oot, though he cannae really get that near 'cause o' the heat, the sea of molten wax goes everywhere, together wi' his wallies...

There is a simple wee trick to remove candle wax drips from carpets and fabric, but it does take a bit of patience. First, wait until the wax has hardened. You can put small garments in the freezer if you have one to speed this up. Scrape up as much of the lump or lumps of wax as you can, using the blunt side of a kitchen knife. Place a sheet of Horace's blotting paper, or if you have no blotting paper, kitchen roll, over the mark. Heat your iron to a warm setting (not too hot or you risk burning the paper) and press lightly down, just briefly. As soon as one area of the paper becomes soaked with the wax, move another bit over the mark and repeat the process. Keep goin' like this until nae mair wax is being sucked oot by the paper.

On tight woven fabrics, this should be enough to remove all the wax, and you should be able to go on and clean the article as normal. However, on looser-woven fabrics or carpets, some wax might stay behind, so you can use a little diluted methylated spirit to finish off the process, but take care and not fade the colour of the fabric.

Better still, get twa o' thae candles that are numbers ! Saves a lot of bother, and fewer cakes tae bake for Blue Watch at the fire station!

Chewing Gum

Chewing gum seems to be a fact o' life these days. It comes in a packet that has bits o' silver wrapping paper fowk they could wrap it up an' bin it, but it seems that chewing gum has a will of its own, and becomes entangled and squished in the most annoying places. Gum can be removed again. It is almost impossible to remove gum when it is warm, so to remove chewing gum from a carpet, or a skirt, or your shoe, you need to harden it.

The easiest way is to use an ice cube. Rub it on the gum 'til it's hard. If the item is wee enough, you can put it in the freezer until the gum has hardened. then you can scrape it off wi' a blunt knife.

There are some clever products in the shops that are specifically intended for the removal of chewing gum from fabrics. They are certainly worth a try, but read the instructions carefully before you decide to buy, to check whether the product is safe to use on the fabric that you are treating.

If you get gum stuck in your hair, you cannae really stick your heid in the freezer. Instead, work a wee bit cooking oil or peanut butter into the gum and hair, then pick or comb the gum out. Ouch!

The only painless and truly effective means of removing chewing gum from hair is cutting it oot ! Then borrow ane o' Paw's bunnets for a week or so. We afternoon tea ladies think that Auchentogle should be like Singapore. We had a visitor fae there no' that long ago. An awfy nice person, Shirley Hew is her name, came for tea and tellt us that chewing gum is banned in Singapore where she comes fae.

Chocolate

This is one thing that bairns somehow manage to get everywhere. Cannae understand how if they like it so much that they can allow one wee crumb to escape - but there we are. Luckily, the results are never that drastic.

Gently scrape up any excess chocolate wi' the back o' a knife or the edge o' a spoon. Dabbing the stain with lukewarm water and detergent will help to loosen it before washing. Most modern washing powders will be able to remove the stain in a machine wash in one go.

Non-washable fabrics can be gently dabbed wi' a sponge an' lukewarm water, but there may well be a grease mark left, so dry-cleaning is next.

Carpets should be rubbed gently with soap and lukewarm water; take care no' to soak the area. Rinse with repeated small amounts of water until you are sure the soap has been removed.

Coffee stains

Fresh coffee stains are quite easy. On washable fabrics, a wee soak in detergent and water is the right way before washing. Black coffee leaves a darker mark, of course. Fresh black coffee stains on carpets or clothing can be removed with soda water if you have any in the house. We used tae hae a soda water fountain-syphon thing that worked wi' cartridges - wonder where that's gone ? Last seen, Hen wis scooshing it doon the back o' Daphne's neck.

Blot up the excess spillage then dab the mark with warm water and a little detergent should be just fine, but you'll just need tae be patient. Remember, always when treating your rugs, try to use the minimum amount of water necessary for the task.

Older stains on washable items can be treated by rubbing glycerine into the stain and leaving it for a while to loosen, then soaking the article in a solution of warm water and borax.

Older stains on carpets may require the use of a carpet-cleaning solution from the shops. You can hire special cleanin' kit. Just be sure you are there tae supervise if you get the menfolk tae help. They will use too much o' everythin', and just cannae grasp that sometimes less is more.

If you reach desperation and you think that the fabric can stand the heat, try pouring boiling water through the stain. This may shift the apparently impossible.

Cream Stains

Marks made by cream spilled on washable claes will often come out completely if washed quickly enough, but sometimes a greasy mark may be left behind. These marks can be removed with a dry-cleaning solution, dabbed on or, if you have an aerosol tin, lightly sprayed onto the area. Methylated spirit can also be handy in removing greasy marks left by cream, but you run risk of damaging the fabric if it is artificial. If you do choose to try methylated spirit, dilute a small amount with an equal quantity of water and see if it works with this before using it neat.

Greasy marks on carpets can be sponged with warm water and borax, or treated with dry-cleaning solution or carpet cleaner in aerosol form.

Curry

We love a curry, but the spices used in cooking curry are responsible for some awfy stubborn stains. Scrape off any excess spillage, then gently dab a half-and-half solution of warm water and glycerine through the fabric, working from the wrong side. This should help to loosen it. Rinse in warm water, then wash, using a biological powder. Stains on white cotton and linen should disaapear by soaking them in a bleach solution, according to the instructions on the bottle.

Try treating non-washable items and carpets by dabbing with a solution of two tablespoons of borax and one litre of warm water. A more drastic alternative is to dab on a little methylated spirit, but try it diluted first, and carry out a spot-test on a spare piece of carpet first if possible.

Maw (Amma) Kumar up the road says that curry stains are easy to remove. She rubs the stains with ordinary soap and places the fabric in the sun to dry. The stain takes on a pink shade. Then, she says, wash it in the usual way, and if that disnae work, dab wi' lemon juiceand leave it in the sun.

Crayon marks

The bairns love to draw. It's the only time you'll get a wee bit o' peace - when they're readin' or drawin'. But crayon marks can be awfy hard to get off some fabrics. You'll need to look at the label on the clothes. On fabrics that do not contain a high proportion of man-made fibres, dab a little methylated spirit onto the stain before washing it as normal, and this might dae the trick. Marks made with wax crayon can also be treated wi' grease solvent or dry-cleaning fluid. You can try the iron and blotting paper method - same as you do for candle wax, but this might still leave some of the mark behind.
Methylated spirit might work on this.

Cycle oil

They're aye oilin' their bikes in this family ! They say it makes them go faster ! If the mark is not too deep in the fabric, it may well come out if it is washed in the machine with a biological washing powder. Dabbing the fabric with soap before washing should help shift the grease. Soften the soap under warm water first, and this will make it easier to work it into the stain.

C is the cycle to ride round the yard

If the mark appears to be right deep down and is not fresh, pre-soaking the article in a borax solution might help you, or you can try givin' the stain a wee dab with methylated spirit before washing, if the fabric is suitable for such treatment.

There's a tin o' stuff that mechanics use tae get motor oil aff their hands. It pongs a bit, but my - it's rare. Keep a wee tin under the sink.

Deodorant

Some o' these deodorants that you buy in the shops can leave a nasty scummy white mark on your clothes, which can build up over a period of time no matter how often you wash them. Mix up a paste of bicarbonate of soda and water and apply this to the marks, rubbing it in gently with your fingers. Leave this mixture on for half an hour or so, then soak the clothes for a while in salty water. Rinse then wash as normal. We used tae make our own deodorants. There's a recipe in my mither's notebook for Astringent deodorant. It works a treat !

Dye runs

Dye runs on white or very pale-coloured washable fabrics can be sorted by soaking the garments in a weak solution of household bleach and water - always follow the instructions on the bottle remember. There are products in the shops specially made to deal with the problem of dye runs, but if you are considering trying such a product, check before you buy.

Egg stains

Egg stains on fabric should be soaked in a solution of detergent and water as soon as possible, and then washed, preferably with a biological washing powder. Do not use hot water for soaking as this will only cook the egg and make it more difficult to shift! If you have been unable to catch the stain while it is still fresh, use a solution of borax and water (two tablespoons of borax to one litre of water) for soaking the article. Sometimes I think Paw should hae his soft biled eggs withoot ony claes on at a', he's that much o' a slitter, but maybe no' come tae think o' it.

Fizzy drinks

The food dyes that are used in the makin' o' some fizzy drinks can leave demons o' stains. When tackling stains on washable fabrics, rinse as much out as possible with lukewarm water, then dab the area with ammonia. Or, try soaking the fabric in water with hydrogen peroxide; use 20 per cent volume hydrogen peroxide diluted with an equal quantity of water. Leave to soak for about fifteen minutes. White cottons can be soaked in bleach solution, according to the manufacturer's instructions.

On carpets, blot up excess spillage on carpets with kitchen roll, then work on the stain with warm water and white vinegar, then ban folk fae drinking ginger in the hoose.

Flatulence

Flatulence is a wee problem for the auld yins. They can get quite upset aboot it. Some of the most common causes are fizzy drinks or just eating too quickly, or chewing with your mouth open, which Granpaw does because of his wallies, or eating too much high fibre - Granpaw loves his cabbage and beans and broccoli, and he eats a lot of bananas, but he has cut these down. Lemons, sweet peppers and yoghurt can be used to help. Lemon juice, mixed with $\frac{1}{2}$ teaspoon of baking soda in water can really help cut out that bloated and cramped feeling.

Vegetables that are high in vitamin C, like sweet peppers, reduce the amount of gas produced in your intestines, but a vitamin C tablet can have the opposite effect.

Yoghurt, as long as it contains acidophilus (a general name for a group of probiotics), uses bacteria that keeps your digestive system normal so that food doesn't linger too long in your intestines and give off excess gas.

There are of course herbal remedies and some spices can help too. Peppermint, fennel, caraway and anise all contain properties that will relieve the problem, and spices like cloves, coriander, dill, rosemary, turmeric, cardamom and basil will do the trick as well.

You can use dried peppermint leaves as a tea - pour on boiling water and leave it to sit for ten minutes, and strain it and drink it warm. You can use crushed fennel, dill oil or leaves, but be careful with the anise in case you get a wee allergic reaction.

Caraway seeds are good too - crushed and made into a tea, or you can get cracker biscuits with caraway.

You can add basil to a lot of dishes - it helps digestion I add rosemary to Granpaw's broccoli, cabbage and beans which helps reduce their gassy effect. Turmeric in rice if you have it on the side helps too, and he loves his rice pudding with fruit, so that gets a few cloves in with it. Coriander goes well in a stir-fry and cardamom is great with vegetables - All these things help.

Fly Marks on a Silk Shade - (Mrs Murphy's tips)

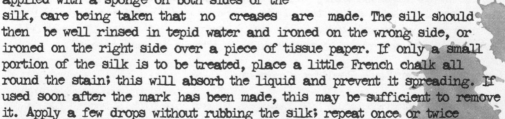

F is for flies that that buzz in the sky

That lamp in the living room seems to attract the flies. This is a good recipe for removing fly marks from coloured silk : $\frac{1}{4}$ lb. soft soap, 1 teaspoonful of brandy, $\frac{1}{2}$ pint of methylated spirit, $\frac{1}{2}$ pint of water. These ingredients should be very well mixed, and applied with a sponge on both sides of the silk, care being taken that no creases are made. The silk should then be well rinsed in tepid water and ironed on the wrong side, or ironed on the right side over a piece of tissue paper. If only a small portion of the silk is to be treated, place a little French chalk all round the stain; this will absorb the liquid and prevent it spreading. If used soon after the mark has been made, this may be sufficient to remove it. Apply a few drops without rubbing the silk; repeat once or twice

Fruit stains - Mrs McSpey swears by this

Soft fruits are the main culprits here, and it is important to try to treat these stains as quickly as possible. On fabrics that can tolerate such harsh treatment, you can try pouring boiling water through the stain -

simple but surprisingly effective! Fresh stains should respond to a brief soak in warm water and detergent, followed by a normal wash with a biological powder. If soaking does not appear to be shifting the stain, you can try dabbing lemon juice onto the area and leaving it for a while before washing.

If the fabric is unsuitable for soaking, dab it gently with a clean pad soaked in borax solution. If this proves unsuccessful, try dabbing it with white vinegar or lemon juice. Carpets can also be treated in this way. Rinse carefully after treatment.

On non-washable items, sponge off the worst with cold water and then either use a proprietary dry-cleaning product or take the article to be professionally cleaned.

If you have been picking or working with soft fruit and your hands have become stained, try rubbing them with lemon juice and salt before washing. This should remove the unsightly marks.

Glue marks by Mrs McNab

There are very many different types of glue available in the shops, each with its own chemical make-up. If you have the container in which the glue was supplied, the first thing to do is to read the instructions carefully to see whether any advice is given on removal methods.

Many of the glues that are recommended for children's use are now washable. Don't however, expect muckle dollops of glue to wash out of fabrics first time without some prior treatment. It is best to try to lift off as much as you can by hand; this can be quite tricky with looser woven or knitted fabrics. Then try to soften the glue with warm water and detergent, dabbing through gently from the reverse side of the fabric, before washing.

For non-washable glues, there may in fact be a solvent available from the manufacturer; use as little as possible to minimize the risk of damage to the fabric. Where no proprietary solvent is available, you can try using methylated spirit, amyl acetate, or white spirit. Where drastic measures are required, you may try paintbrush cleaner or paint stripper, but there is great risk of damaging your material, so this really has to be a last resort.

Grass Stains on Paw's Bowling Flannels

What I don't understand is how Paw gets himsel' in such a mess. You're no' supposed to be rolling aboot on the green - but judgin' fae his troosers he spends a lot o' time just sittin' aboot, and the rest o' it he seems to spend walking on his knees. To remove these stains, put on a solution of equal parts of glycerine and yolk of egg. Let it sit there on the stain for an hour, then wash, and the stain will come out quite easily. Cotton fabrics can be safely treated by gently dabbing methylated spirit onto the stain. This treatment is not recommended for use on man-made fibres. Fabrics requiring milder treatment need a paste of detergent and warm water rubbed gently into the stain prior to soaking in detergent solution. Then, rinse and wash just as normal. Fabrics with any sort of special finish are best sent for dry-cleaning. Treat grass stains as soon as possible to hae the best chance of gettin' rid o' them.

Gravy stains Mrs McSwell says :

Most gravy stains can be removed from washable fabrics by pre-soaking the article in detergent and water solution, then washing it using a good biological washing powder.

Non-washable fabrics should be sponged gently with lukewarm water and detergent; this may well leave a grease stain still to be removed.

Grease Stains - the very dab !

The best way to remove grease spots from light, delicate materials is by using oil of eucalyptus. Put a small quantity on a piece of cotton-wool and gently dab the grease spot; then lay the garment aside to dry, and you might well find that the spot has disappeared, as if by magic ! If it is a really hard stain, a second go might be necessary. I have found this a right grand answer. It leaves no mark on the material, as so many other grease-removers do.

G is for goose with a big yellow beak

Mrs Gow says - Lift off any excess gently, using the blunt edge of a knife. Talcum powder or fuller's earth, sprinkled onto the area and left for a while, should help to absorb the grease. On washable fabrics, soften some soap under warm water and rub this gently into the mark before washing, preferably with a biological washing powder.

It is more difficult to wash grease stains out of carpets without soaking them. You can use fuller's earth or talcum powder and then vacuum it off, then once the excess has been absorbed, you can try sponging it with borax and warm water, then rinsing carefully with repeated small amounts of water. On large stains, however, like last Christmas Day in our house, when the whole turkey, not that long out the oven couped across the floor, it is probably better to use a proprietary carpet cleaner, and not use coloured party hats from the Christmas crackers to try and mop up hot grease.

Methylated spirit can be used on grease marks, but there is a risk of fading the colour, or, on some man-made fabrics, of damaging the fabric itself. Try using it diluted with water first; only if that fails should you resort to using it neat. If you have a sample of fabric or carpet on

which you can carry out a spot-test, it is advisable to do this before you use
something as strong as methylated spirits.

Dry-clean-only fabrics can be treated gently with methylated spirit, but you
are probably safer to use a dry-cleaning spray, or to take the article for
professional cleaning.

Hair spray

Hair spray can stain clothing if used carelessly. Maggie uses enough o' it at
Number 10, then Horace started gettin' on at her about the Ozone - Horace's
homework can be quite interestin' sometimes. Hair sprays used to contain
chlorofluorocarbons (CFCs) as a propellant he says. CFCs are bad for the ozone
layer. That's why they were were banned. But a gentle sponging with borax
solution is usually enough to remove the mark fae claes. It can also leave a
sticky mess on mirrors, but this should come off with hot water and vinegar. I
wish the Ozone was that easy tae fix !

Hangover

Sometimes, I just let them suffer, but mair often than no' I take pity on them,
'cause I can't stand the grumps aboot the hoose.

Eating raw cabbage was an old cure for hangovers. Rosemary was also an old
remedy. Drinking a lot of water was also thought to be an effective cure, and
some folk swallow raw beaten eggs.

Get them oot the hoose - intae the fresh air ! Silly auld fools !

Ink Stains

I get cross at Horace and I shouldn't - He's aye doin' his homework at the
corner o' the living room table after tea. He spreads himsel' oot, pens an' a' and
writes and draws his maps. He tries ever so hard, but the ink goes everywhere.
If I catch him, I get him to put a newspaper down to lean on. But, to remove ink
stains from white articles-linen, calico, etc.-cover the mark well, before
washing with mixed mustard, allowing to it soak in. Then wash and boil in the
usual way, and all traces of the ink will have disappeared. I have tried this
with some really bad stains, and have always found it effective. Horace is going
to be a poet.

More About Ink Stains   from Mrs Jones

If used before the stains have time to dry, methylated spirit will remove ink
at once from carpets and woollen materials. Rub it on with a rag, which will
absorb the ink, first putting a cloth under the material to be treated.

Ink - fountain pen

Many brands of ink for fountain pens are washable nowadays. On carpets, or fabrics where a large quantity of ink has been spilt, pour some salt onto the stain while it is wet and leave it until it has soaked up the ink. Then brush the salt off carefully, making sure that you do not rub any of it back into the fabric in the process. Thereafter, wash fabrics on the hottest wash permissible. Carpets can be dabbed with a half-and-half mixture of white vinegar and warm water.

If the treatments above do not work, then you may like to try the treatments that have been recommended for ballpoint pen stains or to try using one of the stain-specific cleaning solutions that are available in the shops.

Although it is perhaps safe to say that most fountain pen inks are removable, Indian ink may well not be possible to remove.

Ink stains - ballpoint pen

Inks that are used in ballpoint pens vary, so it is safest to start with soap and water when treating a ballpoint stain. Ordinary hand soap, softened under warm water and then pressed gently through the material, can help to shift the stain before rinsing. Make sure that the water that you use is neither too hot nor too cold to avoid the risk of setting the stain.

If this is unsuccessful, try dabbing hot milk through the stain, or stretching the stained part of the fabric over a beaker and pouring the hot milk through it. Do not use the hot-milk treatment on wool, as you could cause matting and shrinkage. Neither is this treatment recommended for carpets. Unless you can be absolutely sure of being able to rinse the milk out properly, you will be left with a most unpleasant smell!

Methylated spirit is a last resort. It can certainly shift the stain fairly quickly, but it may prove to be equally good at removing some of the colour from the fabric! If you are treating man-made fabric, it is safest to dilute the methylated spirit, one part spirit to two parts water, to minimize the risk of damage to the material. If you have no methylated spirit, you can try dabbing a little white spirit onto the stain.

Ink stains - felt tip pens

Many felt-tip pens, especially those produced for the children's market, are washable. Marks left by such pens should respond quite readily to a soak in a solution of detergent and warm water, followed by a wash with biological powder.

If you are unsure as to whether the pen that made the mark is washable or not, you may like to try treating the mark either by dabbing it with methylated spirit, applied with a clean white pad of fabric, or by treating it with a dry-cleaning solution, according to the manufacturer's instructions. However, it is important that you ensure that the fabric that you are treating is unlikely to be damaged by the use of these substances. Red ink is notoriously more difficult to remove than others; you may have to resort to using methylated spirit where this is the culprit. The only time to despair, however, is if the stain has been made by permanent marker pen. Removal will probably be impossible; opting for camouflage instead is probably a better course of action.

Ketchup (Tomato Sauce) stain

It must have been a man who thought up puttin' tomato sauce in a bottle wi' a wee neck on it, so that ye have tae batter it till the palm o' yer hand hurts tae get the wee'est drap oot ! And 9 times oot o' 10 it disnae land onywhere near the plate !

It must have been a man who thought up puttin' tomato sauce in a squeezey bottle so that a fine jet o' sauce can fly across a table and drench all in its path.

But, if you catch stains made by tomato ketchup quickly enough, you should be able to sort them oot by dabbing them with warm water and detergent. Washable items can be soaked for a while in water and detergent before washing.

You need to treat older stains by rubbing glycerine into the material to loosen the stain and leaving it for a while before soaking and washing, or simply washing. Use a biological washing powder for washing, preferably.

Sponge non-washable items and carpets with water and borax, or use a specialist cleaning product.

Lavender; Blue dilly dilly

Lavender is a wonderful thing to have handy.

You can make an insect repellent really easily by mixing a few drops with some sunflower oil, then rub it onto your skin. You can add a wee bit of aloe vera.

Moths are always a problem in Glebe Street, and there's something about the old cedar mothballs that everybody uses that you and your clothes end up smellin' like mothballs ! It's much nicer to have your clothes smelling of Lavender isn't it ? Put sachets of dried lavender buds in your drawers and wardrobes. It fair does the trick.

If you get that stuffed-up feeling, perhaps the early sign of a cold comin' on, an alternative to menthol crystals is to add 4 or 5 drops of essential lavender oil to a bowl of steaming hot water and inhale. Put a towel over your head to catch the steam, breathe in through your nose and you'll clear your passages in no time.

Lavender oil soothes those wee burns that you get in the kitchen - place 2 or 3 drops of lavender oil on the burn and then run it under the tap with cold water.

We were talking about using vinegar to relieve mild sunburn - Another idea is to mix some lavender oil with mineral water and spray it onto your skin. There's nothing like a good night's sleep ! Sometimes I think it's the only peace I get around here ! I sprinkle a few drops of lavender on my pillow - I love the aroma and it really helps me relax. Essential oil of lavender is an antiseptic and it is also an anti-inflammatory.

Next time you have a headache, rub a few drops onto your temples.

Don't forget that you can add lavender flowers to recipes. Lavender chicken is a favourite with us.

Lemons are Magic - We all joined in wi' this one !

Lemons are very useful things , not just for cooking with, but you can use them in so many other ways.

If you are cooking fish in water, a wee drop lemon juice added in will keep the fish from breaking.

If you are boiling old potatoes they'll be whiter if a few drops of lemon juice are added to the water.

When you are poaching eggs, add a little lemon juice to the water and they will not separate.

Lemon juice in stews adds a real bit o' taste and makes the meat more tender.

If you are boilin' meat, a teaspoonful of lemon juice added to the water will prevent it being tough.

F is for
fruit that
is juicy and fresh

Lemon juice added to fresh milk will sour it if you need that for baking.

Dried fruits, prunes, figs, apricots, and the like are improved if a little lemon juice and grated rind or a slice or two of lemon are stewed with them.

Did you know that lemon juice can be used instead of vinegar in all recipes ? (except pickling of course).

You can stop bananas and pears going dark when you cut them if a little lemon juice is sprinkled over them.

Rub a little lemon juice over your hands after washing the dishes -it will keep them soft.

Squeezed-out lemons can also be used to clean white wooden table tops and draining boards. Clean them first, then rub the lemon over them, then rinse.

Lemon juice is good for your hair after a shampoo. Rinse with a solution of water and a little lemon juice.

Lemon juice and water makes a good mouth wash.

Equal portions of lemon juice and glycerine are excellent for soothing a cough.

The same mixture makes a good softening lotion for hard working hands.

Aluminium trays and pans can be cleaned with a cloth dipped in lemon juice, then rinsed in warm water.

Tarnished copper and brass can be cleaned by squeezed-out halves of lemons dipped in salt.

Lemon juice itself is excellent for cleaning brass, copper and aluminium and for getting glassware really bright

Iron rust stains can be removed if the spots are rubbed with lemon juice then covered with salt. Dry in the sun. Repeat the process if necessary.

Grated lemon peel (the yellow portion only should be removed) makes a grand flavouring for cakes and puddings.

Lemons will keep for three months if you store them in air-tight screwtop jars.

You can keep lemons firm and fresh if you put them in wide-mouthed jars and cover them with cold water. (Handy to know if you are tempted by all thae multi-buys in the shops these days.)

Did you know that if you heat a lemon before you squeeze it, you'll get more juice out of it?

Lipstick marks by Jessie

Lipstick is a greasy stain; treat the grease first. Dab it gently with either washing-up liquid or softened toilet soap. This should loosen the grease before washing. Alternatively, you can apply a little eucalyptus oil to break down the grease. If you are left with some colour staining after washing, you may try a little white spirit on the mark, or, on white cotton fabrics, you can try bleach, diluted with cold water according to the manufacturer's instructions.

Non-washable fabrics should be taken to the dry-cleaner's as quickly as possible.

Mildew Stains on White Articles - Bella Mackay's top tip

How many times when my boy has lost last season's sports gear do I find his bag stuffed under his bed and when I go to sort it all out - there's mildew on his shorts !

Here's what you do : Mix equal quantities of soft soap and white starch, and half the quantity of common salt, with the juice of a lemon. Cover the spots of mildew thickly with this mixture, then place the articles in the open air on grass, in sunshine, if possible. Allow to remain for at least a couple of hours, then wash with soap, boil, and rinse well.

Mildew is quite difficult to remove, but there are a few alternative ways of treating it. White washable fabrics may well respond successfully to soaking in bleach solution before washing. Coloured fabrics can be rubbed gently with a paste made from salt and a little water, then soaked in salty water before washing. Another option is to soak the fabric in a weak solution of hydrogen peroxide before washing. Dilute 20 per cent volume strength hydrogen peroxide with an equal amount of water and use this.

Mildew on carpets is probably best left to the experts; unless it is successfully removed, it will only spread. Mildew thrives in damp conditions; thus it can be found in places such as poorly-ventilated bathrooms. Unless the cause of the mildew forming on your carpets, i.e. the damp conditions, are attended to, the problem will only repeat itself.

Mildew on paintwork and tile grout may be removed with a bleach solution, or by using a mildew-removing product, available from any DIY store or ironmonger's.

M is the milk that we drink in the morning

Milk stains - Mrs McNab knows the very thing!

Milk generally does not cause a problem stain unless it is particularly creamy. Most milk stains can be removed very easily by either sponging them with warm water and detergent or giving the article a brief soak in water and detergent before washing. If the stain looks greasy, you can, if you wish, dab it with a little diluted methylated spirit.

The problem with milk is that spillages on carpets can leave an unpleasant lingering smell. Try to be as sure as you possibly can that all trace of the milk has been removed and that the area has been well rinsed. Carpets should be rinsed with repeated applications of small amounts of water. Blot up the water in between rinses to avoid the area becoming too wet.

Nail varnish

Nail varnish remover will be effective in shifting nail varnish from some fabrics, but the acetone in this product will damage fabrics that contain acetate. If you are at all unsure of the fibre content of the fabric that you are treating, use amyl acetate instead. Amyl acetate should be available from your chemist. Spot-test the fabric first, if possible, for colour fading. If you are at all worried that the colour of the fabric might fade, take the garment to a specialist dry-cleaner instead.

There may be some colour staining left after the varnish is removed; treat this cautiously with diluted methylated spirit.

Nail varnish that has been spilt on a non-absorbent surface such as a vinyl floor should be left to dry and then gently peeled off.

Nicotine marks - Aggie Pry's solution

If there is a smoker in your house, curtains will have to be washed or dry-cleaned regularly to keep them fresh and free of nicotine stains. Unless they are cleaned regularly, a build-up of nicotine staining is inevitable, collecting especially around the pleats at the top, and there will be little you can do to restore the curtains to their proper colours. Unless the smoking can be stopped, choosing darker colours for your curtain fabrics is the best means of disguising the staining, although regular cleaning will still be necessary to keep the curtains smelling fresh.

Staining on washable walls and wallpapers can be treated with a solution of sugar soap and water; this will do much to improve matters. Unfortunately on non-washable wallpapers there is little you can do.

Nicotine stains on fingers can be removed by rubbing them with lemon juice before washing with soap and water.

The perfect solution ? NO SMOKIN' IN THE HOOSE.

Paint - Acrylic - Mrs Jones is oor expert aboot paints

Acrylic paint will come out of fabrics and carpets without any problem if you catch it while it is wet. You need only use cold water and it should rinse out quite easily. It may be possible to pick hardened acrylic paint off fabrics, but failing that, you may have to resort to paintbrush cleaning fluid and risk damaging the fabric.

Paint - Emulsion

Emulsion paint is a classic example of a stain that can be removed easily when fresh. Unfortunately, it is well-nigh impossible to get out once the paint has dried!

While the paint is still wet, sponge the affected area of fabric as generously as you dare with warm water. Work from the reverse side of the fabric if possible, trying to push the stain back out. Then work on the stain using warm water and a generous quantity of detergent. When you are confident that the stain is almost out, rinse thoroughly then wash in the normal manner.

Carpets should be treated with detergent and water, but care must be taken not to soak the area.

Older stains are really tricky; you can try paintbrush cleaning solution, but this can be very dangerous to all but the most hardy of fabrics.

Paint - Oil based Gloss and enamel

These stains are best caught fresh. Whenever you are decorating at home, or using gloss or enamel paint for any project, have a bottle of white spirit or turpentine and some clean rags to hand. You are sure to need them!

Dab the affected area with a clean pad of fabric dipped in white spirit or turpentine. Use as little spirit as possible in order to remove the stain without damaging the fabric.

Dry gloss paint can be treated with paintbrush cleaner, but this is a very strong solvent, and it is used only at great risk to the fabric being treated.

Great care should be used with white spirit, turpentine and paintbrush cleaner. Never smoke when you are using them, and keep the area in which you are working well ventilated.

Paint - Poster

Poster paint is generally thought to be washable, but sometimes some colours, red in particular, can leave a stain. You can try treating washable items with hydrogen peroxide solution, 20 per cent volume strength, diluted with the same quantity of water. Leave the article in this solution for about fifteen minutes and then wash as usual. Spot-test this solution on coloured articles before use.

Perspiration marks

Perspiration marks on white cotton garments can be shifted by soaking in a bleach solution, according to the manufacturer's instructions. Or, you can try dabbing the marks with ammonia, white vinegar or lemon juice. Rinse out, then wash as normal.

Pianos

We have that many parties and celebrations here at No 10 - seems like there's always a birthday or folk dropping in on Burns' night or whatever, and we all like a good tune and a sing-song, so our old piano is important.

Did you know that pianos are very sensitive to changes of temperature. They should be placed away from draughts. Upright pianos sound better if placed about two inches from the wall, and an inside wall is preferable.

If you use glass or mahogany cups under the castors of your piano, it will spread the weight of the instrument over a larger floor space thus avoiding dents in the carpet.

When not in use, the keyboard of a piano should be kept closed. Not only is it important to keep pianos free from dust, but great care should also be taken to see that pins and needles are not placed on them. They are apt to get inside and your melodies will rattle.

 The tops of pianos shouldn't be loaded with photographs, ornaments and the like, as the tone will be deadened, but the way Joe thumps the piano, it doesn't make much difference to us, but if you are trying some classical stuff then bear it in mind.

Pianos must be tuned at regular intervals even if they are not frequently in use.

Piano keys will turn yellow if washed with water. Wipe them with a soft cloth soaked in methylated spirits then polish with a dry cloth or chamois leather.

Rust - Mrs Murphy says . . . . .

Lemon juice and salt are your best pals when trying to remove rust marks from articles of clothing. Saturate the stain with the lemon juice, then sprinkle on a generous amount of salt. Leave this to work on the stain for a short while; if you can spread it out in the sunlight, so much the better. Thereafter, rinse out the article and wash as normal.

Rust marks on carpets are best treated with proprietary carpet-cleaning products, but if the mark is only a slight one, it may come out with lemon juice diluted with water.

Scorch marks

Severe scorching is, unfortunately, probably there to stay, but light scorching can be treated with a half-and-half water and hydrogen peroxide solution dabbed gently onto the fabric. Alternatively, you can try dabbing on a borax solution, or, on suitable fabrics, soaking in bleach solution. After treatment, rinse then wash as normal.

Shoe Polish

Shoe polish can be treated much in the same way as many other greasy stains, such as cycle oil, but you will probably find it hard to remove the colour staining. White spirit or methylated spirit may prove effective but should be used with caution; the colour of the fabric could be altered, and in some cases the fabric could be damaged. Dry-cleaning aerosol sprays can give success but must be used with care.

Silver Cutlery cleaning

We've got my mither's silver cutlery - 12 of everything here at No 10 - and it is all there - not a piece missing, but it gets awfy tarnished.

Mither was aye entertainin' before Faither passed away and things got awfy hard but she was always proud o' the silver !

I get the menfolk to polish it all once in a while, but last time they were all moaning and said they were too busy and tried to hide, but I went out to the shops and left them to it and said there would be no tea if the job wasn't done.

Little did I know that Horace had come up with a plan from his chemistry book that saved them from actually doing any work !

I'll tell you what they did - they took the big pan, lined it with a sheet of aluminium cooking foil, and scrunched up a few into bits the size o' golfballs, and boiled up water in it with 2 tablespoons of salt and 2 tablespoons of baking soda.

Then they plunged the silver cutlery in, so that it was covered in water and lying on the foil.

The tarnish lifts off the silver and moves onto the foil. It needs a soak for 10 minutes. Horace says its a chemical reaction between the aluminium metal and the tarnish (silver sulphate apparently) and the table salt acts as an electrolyte to make the reaction happen.

Then all they had to do was rinse and dry .

Mrs Gow won't do that with her silver - she cleans hers with ordinary toothpaste - she just puts some on a damp cloth - it works a treat.

Snoring - whit a noise !

Paw snores. Everybody complains about it. You can hear it across the landing!

We've had to find ways of stopping him snoring so the street can get some sleep!

123

The main cause of snoring is that the air passage in your throat shrinks and so when you sleep, your body is not getting enough air. Snoring is how your body tries to make up for that.

But the problem is that your tongue gets in the way of the airway, and if you can get your tongue to stay out of the way when you are sleeping this will cut oot the snoring.

Most folk who who snore, breathe through their mouths when they sleep.

I read about a new idea, a chin strap. The idea is that if your mouth is kept shut when you sleep, you are forced to breathe through your nose which means that you will stop snoring. Paw didn't like the elastic attached to one of his old bunnets. Said he couldn't sleep wi' a hat on.

We tried stuff from the chemist - nasal strips (that open the breathing passages) and all sorts of nasal sprays. We got him a special pillow, designed to support his neck better, so that the airway stays open .

But the best answer ? I sewed a wee pocket into the back of his pyjamas and put in a tennis ball into it so he cannae sleep on his back. Peace at last !

Removing Tea Stains from Table Linen

This was what started it all - that afternoon we were discussin' who can bake the lightest sponge, or make the best scones, when Mrs Murphy accidentally started that wee calamity !

It is sometimes very difficult to remove a tea stain from table linen with ordinary washing and boiling, especially if the tea had milk in it and the stain has been there a wee while. In such a case, use a bleaching fluid, but this need not be destructive to the material if properly and carefully used.

There are plenty of bleaches in the shops - but read what it says on the label !

Mrs Gow says to use the bleach, either rub the stain with a piece of soft rag soaked in the bleach solution, or add 1 tablespoonful to 1 pint of cold water and allow the stained part to soak in this for half an hour or less. Rinse thoroughly in cold water.

Stains on Table Linen (Granmaw Broon's Remedy)

If that precious damask tablecloth (the one that Granmaw got as a weddin' present) gets splashed with gravy or fruit, a little French chalk rubbed in at once, left for a few minutes, and then brushed off, will remove the mark.

I always keep a tiny box of it in the sideboard, and use some when accidents occur, often saving having to send a clean cloth from being sent to the laundry.

Tea stains should not be a problem on washable fabrics, if they are treated without delay. Soak the garment or cloth in warm water and detergent, preferably overnight, then wash as normal. Older stains can be soaked overnight in borax solution before washing. Alternatively, dab glycerine onto the fabric, working it into the fibres. Leave this for a while to loosen the stain before washing.

If the fabric is suitable for the hottest wash in the washing machine, this may well be all that is required to remove tea stains.

Non-washable fabrics can be treated with dry-cleaning aerosol (used with caution) or dabbed with a clean pad soaked in borax solution. If you prefer to have the article dry-cleaned, then it should be treated at the earliest opportunity.

Tea stains on carpets must be caught quickly. Soak up excess liquid with kitchen towels, then sponge with water and detergent, or borax solution.

Toothache

Keep a wee bottle of oil of cloves handy. Dab on to the affect area wi' a cotton bud, and get to your dentist!

Vinegar - you could have a whole book - just about vinegar !

The afternoon tea ladies were saying how wonderful lemons were, and I said - 'but lemons are no' a patch on vinegar....'

It's great for carpet stains - if you make a mixture of 1 teaspoon of ordinary liquid detergent with a teaspoon of white distilled vinegar in a pint of lukewarm water, you can shift non-oily stains from the carpet.

Use a bit of an old towel and rub gently. Rinse it out with a bit of towel, damp, but not wringin' with clean water and dab it dry.

Repeat until the stain has vanished, then get Daphne's hair dryer and dry it off.

Washing windows with a mixture of equal parts of white distilled vinegar and warm water. Dry off with a soft cloth to make your windows gleam, and a wee extra tip is to rub-off with a sheet of last week's Sunday Post.

Washing woodwork, painted walls and venetian blinds is easy if you use a mixture of 1 cup ammonia, $\frac{1}{2}$ cup white distilled or cider vinegar and $\frac{1}{4}$ cup baking soda with 1 gallon of warm water. Wipe this on with a sponge or cloth and rinse off with clear water.

Glass or cup marks on wood - These telltale rings from wet glasses being rested on wood furniture can be shifted by rubbing them with a mixture of equal parts of white distilled vinegar and olive oil. Always rub with the grain and then polish.

Vinegar is great for cleaning a microwave oven - all you do is boil a solution of $^1/_4$ cup of white distilled vinegar and 1 cup of water in the microwave. It loosens the splashes of food and deodorizes it at the same time.

To clean your fridge use a solution of water and white distilled vinegar, 50/50.

You can use it to clean and disinfect your wooden chopping boards - Use white distilled vinegar neat !

I use it when it's my turn to polish the brass at the foot of the stair. Brass, copper and pewter will really shine if you clean them with this mixture : Dissolve 1 teaspoon of salt in 1 cup of white distilled vinegar and stir in flour until it becomes a paste. Paint on the paste to the metal and let it stand for about half an hour. Rinse it off with clean warm water and polish dry.

Granpaw uses vinegar to stop ant invasions - they get in at his back door. If you wipe counter tops and floors with neat white distilled vinegar, they'll not bother you.

Bathtub grime can be removed by wiping it down with white distilled vinegar and then with soda. Rinse clean with water though, otherwise you'll not smell so nice for a wee while - and while you're at it, give that shower screen a wipe down with a sponge soaked in white distilled vinegar to take off soapy residue.

It's a weedkiller too ! Granpaw sprays white distilled vinegar (neat) on the tops of weeds.

Mrs Gow says that a drop o' vinegar keeps cut flowers longer. Mix 2 tablespoons of sugar and 2 tablespoons of white vinegar in a vase of water. Make sure you trim the stems and change the water every four or five days.

Vinegar is a paintbrush softener - soak the brush in hot white distilled vinegar, and then wash it out well with warm, soapy water.

Joe uses vinegar on his car when he thinks there is going to be a hard frost next morning. He wipes the windows the night before with a solution of one part water to three parts white distilled vinegar. No need to get the scraper out and be late for work.

You can clean leather shoes with vinegar to get rid of these salty marks - 50/50 water and white vinegar, and use it sparingly - Damp a cloth with the solution, and dab it over.

Vinegar can be used to clean gold jewellery. Best is apple cider vinegar - a cupful, and steep the item for 15 minutes. Remove it and dry it with a soft cloth.

Vinegar even works on worn DVDs - so Maggie says. She says if you have one of those annoying DVD's that sticks, wipe it down gently with white distilled vinegar on a soft cloth. Make sure it's dry before you try it.

Wine stain spots can be removed from 100 percent cotton, cotton polyester and permanent press fabrics if attempted within 24 hours. Gently sponge white distilled vinegar directly onto the stain and rub away the spots. Then clean as normal according to the directions on the label.

Deodorant stains are a bit of a problem at Number 10. These youngsters are awfy conscious of smellin' right, which is no bad thing. Deodorant and antiperspirant stains can be removed from shirts and blouses by lightly rubbing them first with white distilled vinegar and then washing or laundering as normal.

Keeping colours from running - this is a great tip - vinegar is a 'fixer' To hold colours in most fabrics, those which tend to run, soak them for a few minutes in white distilled vinegar before washing them.

Scorch marks on fabrics can be removed if you lightly rub white distilled vinegar on to the part that has been slightly scorched. Wipe off with a clean cloth. You might need to do this a few times - but well worth a try.

Have you been scunnered when you are ironing to see dirty marks appearing on that clean collar or cuff ? Clean your iron plate by heating equal parts white distilled vinegar and salt in a small pan. Rub the solution onto the cooled iron surface to remove dark or burned stains.

The last drop ! There's always a fight at Glebe Street when the sauce bottle is getting empty - eleven round the table - all dowsin' their chips in sauce, hoping there'll be some left - so, before the fight starts, when you can't get the last bit of out of the bottle, pour a little vinegar into it, put the lid on nice and tight and shake well. You'll be amazed at how this keeps the peace !

Boiling eggs sounds easy doesn't it ? Paw cannae dae this without cracking them and losing most of the white - so I tell him to put a little vinegar in the water , and all is well.

If you like fluffy rice add a teaspoon of white distilled vinegar to the boiling water before adding the rice.

Soothe a bee or jellyfish sting with vinegar. Splash it on neat. It will soothe the irritation and relieve itching, and stem the tears !

You can even relieve sunburn by lightly rubbing white distilled or cider vinegar on the skin. You can relieve dry and itchy skin too simply by adding 2 tablespoons of vinegar to a bath.

Hen's remedy for dandruff, is to rinse after shampooing, with a solution of $\frac{1}{2}$ cup vinegar and 2 cups of warm water.

Gargle to soothe a sore throat by putting a teaspoon of vinegar in a glass of water. Gargle, then swallow.

For another great gargle: 1 cup hot water, 2 tablespoons honey, 1 teaspoon vinegar, gargle then drink. Paw swears by a different remedy - hot whisky and honey.

Horace got a wart from the swimming baths. I mixed warm water with a cup of white distilled vinegar and made him sit with his feet in a bowl every day for 20 minutes until the wart disappeared.

Wine stains by Aggie & Nelly Pry (who seem tae ken a' aboot this)

White wine does not present a problem as regards stains; any spillages can be simply blotted up and sponged off with soapy water.

Red wine, especially the darker varieties, can leave a very ugly purple-blue stain if not treated correctly.

Fresh red wine stains can be treated very successfully with white wine if you can afford it; simply pour the white wine onto the stain, wait a couple of moments, and then rinse it away; the red wine marks will disappear as you do so. This method is equally as successful for red wine spillages on carpets as it is on fabrics, but you have to be careful not to pour on too much white wine; apart from the fact that this would be very wasteful, it would leave the carpet very wet and could cause shrinkage.

For those of you who are not in the habit of having a spare bottle of white wine to hand, or who do not like the thought of good wine being frittered away in such a manner, the alternative, salt, is almost as effective and certainly cheaper. Pour enough salt onto the spillage to cover the area completely. As the wine soaks up into the salt, add some more. Keep adding salt until it stops absorbing the wine. Some advocates of this method would recommend sweeping up the salt immediately, but it is better to leave it until the salt is drier, thus avoiding pushing any of the wine back into the fabric as you sweep the salt up.

A third option for treating red wine stains is to soak them in soda water, but this does not guarantee success.

Wine stains that have been left to dry are more of a problem. If all else fails, and you think that the fabric can stand up to it, pour boiling water through the stain and you may finally have some success.

128

129

NEW

Shetland Knitting

Presented with
"PEOPLE'S FRIEND"

"PEOPLE'S FRIEND"

JUMPERS and JACKETS BOOK

NQUHAR

KNITTING BOOK

Presented with
"People's
Friend"

The Paper For
Every
Home

ted With
E'S FRIEND'

Day To Day Diary

Date _____

Remedies & Suchlike

We hae a busy time here at Glebe Street and at the But An' Ben, and there's no' often much peace to yersel'. There's often some kind o' carry-on so I've jotted down some o' the things that made me smile when I remember the wee hints that help us get by. There's some other bits an' pieces too.

Maw

We prefer a carry oot!
- Heu

Date _____ Lavender _____

Housewife's Choice

Lavender's blue, dilly dilly.

Lavender's green

When you are King, dilly dilly.

I shall be Queen

Lavender's broon, dilly dilly.

Lavender's broon

When there's a spill, dilly dilly.

I'll be there soon!

Lavender

Lavandula vera
Occurrence: indigenous to mountainous regions in the western Mediterranean and is cultivated extensively in France, Italy, England and Norway.
Parts used: the flowers and the essential oil which contains linalool, linalyl acetate, cineol, pinene, limonene and tannin.
Medicinal uses: aromatic, carminative, stimulant, nervine. It is mainly used as a flavouring agent for disagreeable odours in ointments or syrups. The essential oil when taken internally is restorative and a tonic against faintness, heart palpitations, giddiness and colic. It raises the spirits, promotes the appetite and dispels flatulence. When applied externally, the oil relieves toothache, neuralgia, sprains and rheumatism. The oil is utilised widely in aromatherapy, often to very beneficial effects.
Administered as: fluid extract, tincture, essential oil, spirit, infusion, tea, poultice, distilled water.

Remedies an' Suchlike
(My favourite things first!)

Lavender Bags

To make your own lavender bags, pick about 20 or so stems of lavender, and leave them to dry for about a week on a tray wi' space between them. You'll need to strip the dried heads off the stems.

You can make a simple lavender bag from any wee pieces of material you might have and either sew them shut after filling, or make a bag with a drawstring ribbon.

The bag wi' a drawstring makes them easier to re-fill. You can choose pure dried lavender, or you can blend it with a wee drop o' dry rice mixed with some drops of lavender oil. Makes a heavier bag.

Lavender

One large handful of dried lavender weighs about 1oz., so a bag about the size of the palm of your hand will take about 1oz.. Use the fragrant lavender for this purpose – it's better than the blue.

Lavender Bags will keep the Moths away :
Awfy things, moths. They go for clothes in your cupboards as they like to live indoors, and make a right good meal o' your natural fibres like wool, and silk. They're awfy hard to get rid o' once they have moved in.

Hang lavender bags in your wardrobe and drawers. They'll do the trick for two or three months, but you need to give them a squeeze from time to time to refresh the fragrance. Freshly dried lavender can replace the old lavender, or add a few drops of essential lavender oil.

Day To Day Diary

Date

A Lavender Poke

I sometimes make a wee poke of lavender — if you've got some window-netting or something like that — about 8 or 10 inches.

Get a big saucer, and draw round it, and cut oot the circle. Thread a good size darning needle and do a running stitch round the edge about 3/4" in, wi' some embroidery thread.

It's better than smellin' o' moth balls!

You can draw in the thread to make a wee poke, leaving a gap at the neck.

Put 2 or 3 teaspoons of dried lavender heads inside, and pull your thread tight and tie it round wi a bow, or finish it off wi' a bit o' ribbon.

135

Lavender: Potpourri

How To Make A Potpourri

You'll need basic ingredients – about 12oz. rose petals and rose buds and 4oz. lavender or some camomile flowers – maybe some pine cones too or other dried flowers that you like.

For the fragrance:

4 or 5 drops each of essential lavender oil and essential rose oil

A fixative to make it last: use orrisroot or gum benzoin.

Here's what to do : Mix the ingredients

with your few drops of essential oil. Add the fixative. Gie it a good shake and store it in a warm dark place for five or six weeks in a glass jar wi' a lid to allow the fragrance to develop. Gie it a shake every two weeks.

Day To Day Diary

Date

Lavender:
Potpourri/pillows

If you're in a rush, you can use a fragrance oil instead, and mix the ingredients up in a plastic bag, and then leave it for a few hours before using it. Just keep in mind the four basic ingredients — flowers for the colour and scent; some spices; the aromatic leaves and a fixer to bind it and keep the fragrance trapped in, then you cannae go far wrong.

Ahh!
Relaxing!

You can use potpourri in your bedroom. Lavender helps you relax and sleep. I have a lavender pillow that I put under my main pillow, and rose is awfy romantic don't you think?

Put some potpourri in the lobby — add dried orange and essential orange oil for a right welcoming citrus smell for a' your visitors.

137

Lavender Bath

Bath Time At Glebe Street!

I have to make sure oor lot are a' done wi' the bathroom before I get peace. There's nothin' worse than just gettin' in to the bath and then hae someone bangin' on the door tae get in.

There's nothing quite like a lavender bath! Hang the poke over the hot tap while you run the water. It's grand to relax in a bath before bedtime.

Make some Thyme Bath Bags for a herbal bath that soothes the skin and relaxes tired and aching muscles. Put some dried thyme in a poke o' cloth. Add some raw oats to make the water soft. Tie it with string and hang it from the hot tap or just let it bob aboot in the water.

Day To Day Diary

Date

Basil / Vinegar Baths

A Bath with Basil (Ha ha!) – Try some dried basil in a poke for a stimulating, reviving and really invigorating bath.

A Vinegar Bath is great if you've got itchy dry skin. Just add a cup of vinegar to your bath water.

Cleans the bath too!

Your favourite essential oils can be used in a bath – just a few drops is all you need – you can choose an oil to match your mood.

Cannae find the Grumpy Oil for you know who!

Ivy, Ground

Glechoma hederacea. Common names: alehoof, gill-go-over-the-ground, haymaids, tun-hoof, hedgemaids, coltsfoot, robin-run-in-the-hedge.
Occurrence: very common on hedges and waste ground all over Britain.
parts used: the whole herb
Medicinal uses: diuretic, astringent, tonic and gently stimulant. It is good in relieving kidney diseases and indigestion. Ground ivy tea is useful in pectoral complaints and in weakness of the digestive organs. The expressed juice, when sniffed up the nose, is said to successfully cure a headache and can be administered externally to ease bruises and black eyes. It also has antiscorbutic qualities.
Administered as: fluid extract, expressed juice and infusion.
DO NOT CONFUSE WITH POISON IVY

139

Pomander Balls

Make A Pomander Ball
(you can get the bairns to help wi' this)
This is what you'll need :
One whole orange or lemon
About 4 oz. whole cloves
One teaspoon ground cloves
One tablespoon of orris root powder

Push the sharp end of the whole cloves into the orange or lemon, and repeat all over it until the fruit is completely covered. Mix up the ground cloves and the orris root together in a bag and drop in the orange or lemon and give it a good shake so that it is well covered with the spices.

Take it out of the bag and wrap it in a piece of tissue paper and put it aside for a fortnight – then tie it with a string and hang it in your cupboard.

If You Cannae Sleep !

Try these if you cannae sleep :

Camomile Tea

SLEEP.
ZiZZZZZ

As a tea, it can help ease nervousness,

depression, headaches too, and help you

sleep.

One ounce of the flowers to 2 pints of

boiling water. Simmer for fifteen minutes

and strain. Emetic when taken warm;

tonic when cold. Dried orange peel added

to camomile flowers, in the proportion of

half the quantity of the flowers, improves

the tonic.

Tarragon Tea

Take a teaspoonful of tarragon and the

same of anise and mix it up in a cup of

boiling water. Leave it for 5 minutes, then

strain it before drinking.

Candles/Harmony
Horace's Poems

<u>Candle Magic</u>
Some folk say that lighting a blue candle
is relaxing as it's a peaceful colour and
brings <u>harmony.</u> I think I'll send some of
our neighbours a whole box for Christmas!

Mrs Gow says –
She has an Aquamarine stone that helps
her to sleep and she says just lookin' at
her Green Tourmaline gemstone helps her
nervous system. I had to look them up in
Horace's science book. I think Diamonds and Pearls
would keep me nice and calm!

If all else fails, get up and
read some o' Horace's Poems!

<u>Juice, Teas and Suchlike</u>
From time to time ane o' oor lot come and
make a fuss about what they need to
eat – if it's not these lassies, Maggie and
Daphne on another diet, it's somebody

Day To Day Diary

Date   *Healthy Juice*

no' feelin' at their best for ane reason or anither, or just needin' a bit comfort food. There's always healthy juice on the go, since Maggie won that 'juicer' at the school raffle. We've tried them a'.

There's just a few recipes that belong here rather than in my main cookbooks. We go through that much tomato sauce and vinegar, but that lot don't know that I make it mysel' and just keep topping up the fancy bottles. That's why these healthier sauce recipes are tucked in here !

Strawberry

Occurrence: found through the whole of the northern hemisphere, excluding the tropics. Parts used: the leaves, which contain cissotanic, malic and citric acids, sugar, mucilage and a volatile aromatic chemical that is, as yet, unidentified. Medicinal uses: laxative, diuretic, astringent. The berries are of great benefit for rheumatic gout while the root is good against diarrhoea. The leaves have similar properties and are used to stop dysentery. Fresh strawberries remove discolouration of the teeth if the juice is left on for about five minutes and then the teeth are cleaned with warm water, to which a pinch of bicarbonate of soda has been added. Sunburn could be relieved by rubbing a cut strawberry over a freshly washed face. Administered as: infusion, fresh berries.

143

Date <u>Juices/ Vegetable</u>
<u>and Fruit</u>

<u>Apple and Carrot Juice</u>

You'll need:

Two apples

One large carrot

2oz. cooked but not pickled beetroot

2oz. white grapes

A small chunk of fresh ginger …and juice!

This is rich in vitamin C. Beetroot is also

grand if you are suffering from constipation

or cystitis, as it is relieves some of the

symptoms.

<u>Spicy Tomato & Celery Juice</u>

For two servings you'll need

6 very ripe tomatoes, about 24oz. and 2

celery sticks

Worcestershire sauce & Tabasco Sauce

Celery salt

Chop and juice the tomatoes and celery. Stir

in the sauces to taste. Pour into glasses with

ice and top with a wee pinch o' celery salt

144

Day To Day Diary

Date

Summer Fruit Juice

You will need:

10oz. strawberries

One nectarine

One eighth slice of honeydew melon

Two or three ice cubes

Blend together and drop in the ice.

Just rare on a summer's day at the But

An' Ben!

Why WAS The wee STRAWBeRRY sad? Because his maw and paw were in a jam!

Summer Salad Drink

You will need:

Three large tomatoes

Half an English garden lettuce

One third of a cucumber

A small handful of fresh parsley

A small clove of garlic (optional)

This is a great way o' usin' up leftover salad bits and is a real thirst-quencher.

Date **Mair Juices**

Daphne's Detox Drink

You will need:

Two sticks of celery

Two carrots

One small cooked, but not pickled, beetroot

One orange, peeled and with the pith removed

One apple

This will make two drinks and it is jist scrumptious. It is also superb for giving your detox a boost, and great for hangovers as it puts all the right vitamins back into your system.

Just don't go adding any salty Worcestershire sauce.

Barley Water

Pearl barley, 2oz.; washed in cold water. Boil in 2 pints of water for a few minutes, strain off the liquid, and throw it away. Then boil the barley in four pints and a half of water, until it is reduced one-half. Add lemon for flavouring.

146

Day To Day Diary

Date <u>Mair Drinks</u>

A Pleasant Effervescent Drink for Heartburn

The juice of an orange, water, and a lump o' sugar to flavour and bicarbonate of soda – about half a teaspoonful. Mix the juice, water, and sugar in a tumbler, then put in the soda and stir.

Apple Water

A tart apple well baked and mashed, and pour on a pint of boiling water. Beat up, cool, and strain. Add a bit o' sugar if desired. This is a rare cooling drink for folk who are a wee bit off-colour.

Ane Twin: Is iT TRue an apple a day Keeps The docTor away? cos I jUsT bRoKe his windae wi' a fiTba!

A Ginger Tea Recipe

4 cups of water

A 2-inch piece of fresh ginger root

Honey and a slice o' lemon

Peel the ginger root and slice it thinly. Boil the water in a pan, add the ginger, cover it and reduce to a simmer for 15-20 minutes. Strain the tea. Add honey and lemon to taste.

147

Vinegars and Ketchups and rain water!

Housewife's Choice

Vinegars and Ketchups

Cheap and Good Vinegar (An old, old recipe!)

To eight gallons of rain water, or distilled water, add six pints of molasses; turn the mixture into a clean, tight, cask, shake it well two or three times, and add three spoonfuls of good yeast; place the cask in a warm place, and in ten or fifteen days add a sheet of common wrapping paper, smeared with molasses, and torn into narrow strips, and you will have good vinegar. The paper is necessary to form the "mother," or life of the vinegar.

Vinegar is really quite cheap to buy these days, so I tend tae make up concoctions wi' herbs and peppercorns and suchlike.
A bottle or two can make a grand gift.
Fruits, such as raspberries, can also gie an edge to a vinegar's taste. These additions leave

Day To Day Diary

Date Vinegars

their flavours and trace amounts of healthy nutrients, too. We're always preserving things for ourselves, but there's nothing nicer than giving a wee gift that didn't cost the earth.

Flavoured Vinegars

I like basil, thyme and oregano.
Lemon balm, nasturtium and dill go well together. You can hae wee adventures! Just be sparin' wi' dill as it's awfy strong.
You'll need :
Clean glass jars with lids
White distilled vinegar, cider or wine vinegar
Your choice of herbs.

Parsley

Carumpetroselinum. Common names: Apiumpetroselinum, Petroselinumlativum, petersylinge, persely, persele.
Occurrence: this was first cultivated in Britain in 1548, now completely naturalized through England and Scotland.
Parts used: the root, seeds and leaves.
The root is slightly aromatic and contains starch mucilage, sugar, volatile oil and apiin. Parsley seeds contain more volatile oil, which consists of terpenes and apiol, an allyl compound.
Medicinal uses: carminative, tonic, aperient, diuretic. A strong decoction of the root is used in gravel, stone, kidney congestion, jaundice and dropsy. Bruised parsley seeds used to be given against plague and intermittent fevers, while the external application of the leaves may help to dispel tumours. A poultice of the leaves is effective against bites and stings of poisonous insects.
Administered as: fluid extract, essential oil, infusion, ointment and poultice.

Date _Vinegars_____

Wash and pat dry the herbs, and fill your jar to the top. Pour the vinegar in over the herbs, filling right to the brim. Put the lid on tight. Put your jars on the window sill for a month, but gie them a wee shake every day. Then, after a month, strain off the herbs and bob's your uncle!

We dinnae hae an Uncle Bob?

Cayenne Vinegar (for Tomato Sauce)
You'll need
1 pint Vinegar
½oz Cayenne Pepper
Put the vinegar into a bottle, with the cayenne. Allow it to stand for a month. Strain off into sterilised bottles with airtight caps, for use when you come to make Tomato Sauce.

Day To Day Diary

Date <u>Tomato Sauce</u>

<u>Tomato Sauce</u>

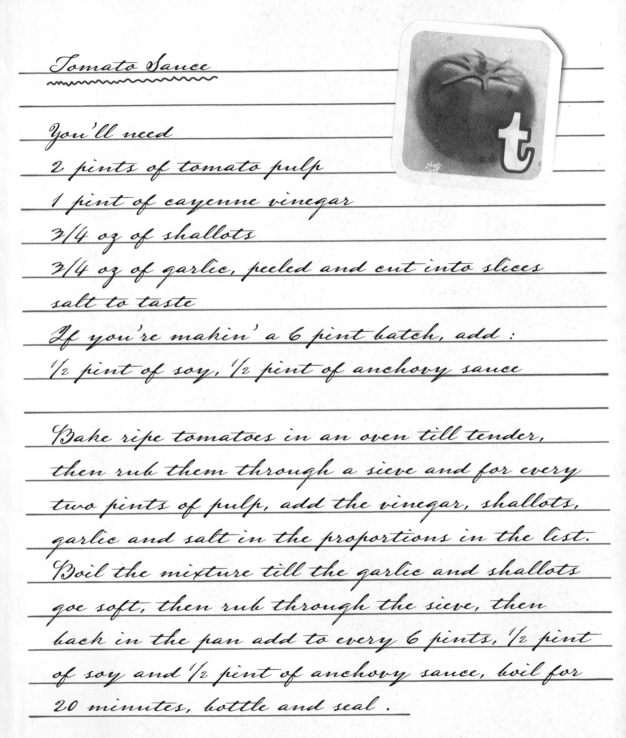

You'll need

2 pints of tomato pulp

1 pint of cayenne vinegar

3/4 oz of shallots

3/4 oz of garlic, peeled and cut into slices

salt to taste

If you're makin' a 6 pint batch, add :

½ pint of soy, ½ pint of anchovy sauce

Bake ripe tomatoes in an oven till tender,
then rub them through a sieve and for every
two pints of pulp, add the vinegar, shallots,
garlic and salt in the proportions in the list.
Boil the mixture till the garlic and shallots
goe soft, then rub through the sieve, then
back in the pan add to every 6 pints, ½ pint
of soy and ½ pint of anchovy sauce, boil for
20 minutes, bottle and seal .

151

Date **Tomatoes**

Housewife's Choice

Vegetable Grower News

The Natural Healing Power Of The Tomato

THE TOMATO is an extraordinary fruit, possessing many health benefits. It can reduce the risk of cardiovascular disease, lowering blood pressure, and reduce the risk of cancer.

Tomatoes are high in nutritional content and rich in Vitamin C, and are a good source of iron and calcium, phosphorus, sulphur and potassium. The tomato also contains amounts of Vitamins A and B. For many, many years tomatoes have been used as home remedies for some ailments.

It is a natural antioxidant, to help your body rid itself of toxins.

• For Acne Scars – Place slices of tomatoes on your face. It is the Vitamin A which helps refresh and rejuvenate.
• For Bloodshot Eyes – have two fresh tomatoes first thing in the morning, before eating anything else.
• For Diarrhoea – if you are suffering from diarrhoea make a juice of tomato paste with water.
• A Face Cleanser – cut tomatoes in half and rub directly onto your skin to purify and cleanse your skin.
• To help with Dark Circles under the Eyes – Mix a paste of 1 tsp tomato juice, ½ tsp lemon juice, a ¼ tsp of turmeric powder with a pinch of gram flour. Apply the paste under your eyes and relax for 10 minutes. Your dark circles will reduce after several applications.
• Ease Sunburn – Steep peeled tomato slices in a cup of buttermilk and place directly on the affected skin. The acidity in the tomatoes closes up your pores and the power of the tomato relieves the discomfort.

• Eczema – Drink tomato juice each day and you will see your skin problems improve.
• Sores and Wounds – In folk medicine, tomatoes were used to heal sores and wounds. Slice a tomato and place it on the sore to clear infections within a few days.
• Mouth Ulcers – to treat mouth ulcers, use tomato juice as a mouth wash, and gargle with the juice three times each day.
• Anaemia – To give relief, drink a blend of tomato and apple juice (50/50).
• Dieting – Tomatoes are low in calories, and useful in dieting because of the essential vitamins and minerals provided.

We've always got tomatoes around – Granpaw grows different varieties, and has won a few prizes in his time. They're awfy guid for ye!

Day To Day Diary

Date Aloe Vera

Hallo Vera!

Hints and Suchlike That Make Me Smile!
"Hallo Vera!"
It wis Maggie that wis goin' on aboot
her to Daphne. I couldn't figure oot
whit she was on aboot – "Hallo Vera!" I
thought we had a new neebor!

The grand thing about Aloe Vera is that
all you need is a wee warm spot to grow
your own aloe plant in a pot. Aloe's a rare
thing to have by you in the kitchen to
treat these nasty wee burns – fae a spurt o'
hot fat, or a hot pot, or grill handle.

It's good for rashes and eczema, dandruff
and acne as well.
These days you see Aloe listed on the
packets o' skin creams and lotions.

Aloe has chrysophanic acid in it which is the magic
healing ingredient – Horace

153

Remedies: Windows

Housewife's Choice

To Mend A Window

Horace was babysittin' and was yellin' oot the windae at the twins tae come in and then slammed the windae shut – ane o' the panes fell oot – bits o' putty everywhere! He and the twins were chewin' gum a' day to get enough tae stick it back in. Naebody noticed till it fell oot again when the frost came.

Hair Cream Substitute

Paw insists on that daft comb-over hair style. He's no got that much left tae comb over. He ran oot o' his haircream so he plastered it wi' a quick mix o' wallpaper paste and dashed oot tae the fitba'. He couldn't get his bunnet aff his heid when he came back.

There's no' even that much tae comb-o'er

Day To Day Diary

Date

When a Table Leg is Shoogly

The big table at the But An' Ben is shoogly at one corner. It's been like that for years. After another spillage though, enough is enough and Paw set about fixin' it. The table was turned upside doon, and each leg precisely measured to within 1/64th of an inch, taking a bit off here, and another bit there. It took a' day. Now it shoogles at twa corners. It wisna' the table it wis the flair!

A Handy Hint About Kettle Handles

A kettle handle can get awfy hot, especially on that gas ring. Best thing is to bind it around wi' string. To make a good job use quite thick string, tying it round at one end with the knot underneath, then bind it around, tucking the end under the last loop and trimming

Sponge Cake/Kippers

Housewife's Choice

it neatly. A coat of varnish will keep it clean. Granpaw made a rare job o' this.

> Does anybody know where we can get a new cord for Maggie's dressing gown?

To Keep A Sponge Cake New

Put a wee slice of bread into the tin. The bread will go as hard as a stone, but the cake will be fresh and spongy for several days. We've never had to use this hint in oor hoose. I've never known a sponge to last more than half an hour.

A Way With Kippers

If you put kippers in a pan, pour boiling water o'er them and cover them wi' a plate, and leave them for ten minutes, they will be cooked perfectly. They swell a bit and are all the tastier.

Well, as Paw says, there's 10 o' us here –

two each for the grown-ups — that's 17 kippers. That's why we used the old urn. It wasn't our fault that Granpaw borrowed it without asking for the bowling club coffee mornin'!

If You Keep Chickens

Vinegar keeps chickens from pecking at each other. The farmer up the road from the But An' Ben puts it in their drinking water.

Is that how you get pickled eggs?

Soap In Emergencies

Granpaw once temporarily stopped up a gas leak by pressing a piece of soap round the pipe where it is escaping while he waited for the gas man.

* With a gas escape call the gas emergency number immediately! *

A creaking door can be silenced by applying soap to the hinges.

The twins excuse for no' using it to wash their necks? "Maw if we used it, whit would you dae in an emergency?"

Date **Motorcycle Cleaning**

Housewife's Choice

Cleaning Grandpaw's Motorcycle and Sidecar

For cleaning the enamel of a motorcycle and sidecar mix up equal quantities of vinegar and linseed oil. Apply a little on a dry cloth, and polish with another cloth. A rub with a duster will then be all that is required to retain the gleam and shine, but he aye uses my cloths – he spends mair time cleanin' that auld bike than he does his ain hoose, and he never lifts a finger round here unless its got a fork or spoon attached!

Asparagus

Asparagus officinalis. Common name: Sparrow grass.
Occurrence: a rare native in Britain, but found wild on the south-west coast of England. It is cultivated as a food crop in parts of Scotland.
Parts used: the root.
Medicinal uses: this plant has diuretic, laxative, cardiac and sedative effects. It is recommended in cases of dropsy.
Administered as: expressed juice, decoction or made in a syrup.

Day To Day Diary

Date <u>Foot Pamperin'</u>

<u>Foot Pamper</u>

To prevent hard skin forming on your feet and to be comfy in hot weather, empty into a shoebox, 4 ozs of boracic powder. Each morning rub the powder into your feet and between the toes, leaving as much on as possible. Also, sprinkle the powder inside the foot of each stocking. You feet will feel soft and smooth in no time.

Aye — and you can follow the footprints a' roon' the hoose. It's like a dancin' class!

I was looking up at the kitchen window — I saw Paw — wavin'. I waved back. But he was that close to the window he must have been sitting in the sink! Somethin' was up! Well, he was sittin' on the drainer wi' his feet in the sink, wi' the hot tap on (runnin' cauld by this time). He'd added a few spoonfuls of baking soda as it filled and was soakin' his sair feet in the baking soda water — supposed tae be for just about 5—10 minutes, but he'd

159

Feet/Crosswords/Gloves Housewife's Choice

been there for three hours with his toe stuck up the cold tap. The auld fool couldn't get the plug oot! His toes looked like prunes by the time we dismantled the tap and lifted him doon.

Writing On Newspaper

If you like a crossword you will find that the ink will not run if the paper is warmed at the fire for a few minutes before writing on it. But, by the time that Paw gets the answer, it doesn't work — so its up and doon — up an doon a' afternoon.

To Prevent Children Losing a Glove

Sew a piece of tape to the gloves, long enough to go from one hand to the other around the neck. When put on before the coat it will not show. In this way gloves will not be lost.

Day To Day Diary

Date Piano Stool

Granpaw watched me do this. He did it with his gardening gloves, with elastic, but couldn't get them through his sleeves so they were outside his jacket, so every time he bent down to pluck a weed it catapulted backwards over the fence to McKay's allotment – who wasn't best pleased.

Another Use For A Piano Stool

A revolving piano stool can be used at the sewing machine instead of a chair. It can be lowered or raised to suit folk of different heights, and you can turn around to reach out for scissors or material etc with ease.

But if you are Ane or Hher Twin, the piano stool is an indoor playground – Ye can birl roon' an' roon' till it stops all of a sudden and get flung aff – and you get up in a giddy spin and knock o'er the aspidistra! Just dinnae get yer fingers caught between the seat bit and the base!

161

Date

Squeaky Piano Pedals/ Hot Water Bottles

Housewife's Choice

If You Have Squeaky Piano Pedals

The front panel of the piano can be removed. Use a lead pencil to rub over the part where the friction occurs.

The other cure is to get the twins to tie Joe's shoelaces together when he is playing the piano.

The Safe Way to Fill A Hot Water Bottle

When filling, lay it flat on the table or drainer beside the sink, holding the neck of the bottle upright. This will prevent the boiling water from spurting over your hand, which is caused by the air being trapped in the bottle if you do it upright. We have 10 hot water bottles, but only 9 stoppers. To make sure of a warm bed, always have a stopper on a string around your neck.

HEN'S

Day To Day Diary

Date *Tacking Carpets*

Tacking Carpets

We were a' helpin' to pit doon the new carpet in the lobby. It was like country dancin'! Shuffling our feet into the corners – and there's a lot o' corners in the lobby. We're a' trying to keep the carpet flat and Hen and Joe are tryin' tae tack it doon – but the hammer either batters the skirting or their fingers. A'body tried. Tacks flyin' – fingers getting sucked and

Foxglove

Digitalis purpurea. Common names: Witch's gloves, dead men's bells, fairy's glove, gloves of Our Lady, bloody fingers, virgin's glove, fairy caps, folk's glove, fairy thimbles, fair women's plant.

Occurrence: indigenous and widely distributed throughout Great Britain and Europe.

Parts used: the leaves, which contain four important glucosides—digitoxin, digitalin, digitalein and digitonin—of which the first three listed are cardiac stimulants.

Medicinal uses: cardiac tonic, sedative, diuretic. Administering digitalis increases the activity of all forms of muscle tissue, particularly the heart and arterioles. It causes a very high rise in blood pressure and the pulse is slowed and becomes regular. Digitalis causes the heart to contract in size, allowing increased blood flow and nutrient delivery to the organ. It also acts on the kidneys and is a good remedy for dropsy, particularly when it is connected with cardiac problems. The drug has benefits in treating internal haemorrhage, epilepsy, inflammatory diseases and delirium tremens. Digitalis has a cumulative action whereby it is liable to accumulate in the body and then have poisonous effects. It should only be used under medical advice. Digitalis is an excellent antidote in aconite poisoning when given as a hypodermic injection.

Administered as: tincture, infusion, powdered leaves, solid extract, injection.

Don't Bang The Door **Housewife's Choice**

shaken in air that was turning blue —
then Granpaw arrives.

He takes the tack — pushes it through a
piece of stiff paper the size o' a 10 bob note,
and holds the paper instead of the tack.
Nae mair bruised fingers!

Don't Bang The Door

That big heavy front door gets into a state
— there's that many folk to-in' and fro-
in', that several pulls are required before it
shuts or opens properly. It's because the
locks are gettin' auld and the hinges are
not takin' the weight properly. Tighten
the hinges — take the weight off them
by jamming a book or a piece of wood
under the door — nice and tight, and
then drive the screws in hard. The book or
wood can be kicked away. Oil the locks.
But — be sure and tell folk. Daphne put

Day To Day Diary

Date *Pearl cleaner*

her shoulder to the door as usual, but met with no resistance at a' and crashed into the lobby, wi' her shopping goin' everywhere.

To Clean Your Best Pearls

Submerge your pearls in a wee tin of powdered magnesia, leave overnight and gently brush off the powder in the morning.

We took them oot and hid them!
Maw thought they'd dissolved!

Rhubarb

Rheum rhaponticum. Common names: Garden rhubarb, bastard rhubarb, sweet round-leaved dock. Occurrence: its cultivation started in England around 1777 and spread throughout Great Britain. It is found growing wild or near dwellings. Parts used: the rhizome and root. The stem and leaves of the plant contain potassium oxalate in quantity and some people are more sensitive to these salts and should avoid eating the plant. People with gout or those subject to urinary irritation should avoid the plant as well.

Medicinal uses: stomachic, aperient, astringent, purgative. This plant has a milder action than its relative, Turkey rhubarb (Rheum palmatum). It has a milder purgative effect and is particularly useful for stomach troubles in infants and looseness of the bowels. In large doses, rhubarb has a laxative effect. A decoction of the seed is proposed to ease stomach pain and increase the appetite. Rhubarb leaves were formerly used as a vegetable in the nineteenth century, and several fatal cases of poisoning were recorded. Administered as: decoction and powdered root.

Varnish the Floor

Housewife's Choice

Floor Varnish Makes Polishing Easier

Varnish the floor working carefully and evenly and plan your retreat so you don't paint yersel' into a corner, as it has to dry completely. But, Horace was doing his homework in the boxroom off the livin' room and was stranded for 24 hours. We had to rig up a pulley system to feed him donuts and onion rings.

A Use For Tea Leaves

Put aside a few days worth o' used tea leaves. Soak them in a pan for half an hour, then strain them and use the liquid for cleaning varnished wood. Tea is a great cleaner – good for windows and mirrors too. Give the leaves to Granpaw for his allotment (for compost) but I wouldn't be surprised if he has another go at gettin' a cup o' tea oot o' them first!

Day To Day Diary

Date **Housework Cap/
Children and Food**

A Cap For Housework

Use an old rubber bathing cap while doing the housework – better than a knotted handkerchief. It stops smells like disinfectant getting into your hair. If someone comes to the door, handy to keep an old wig on the coatstand to avoid scaring the living daylights out of whoever it is.

Children and Food

Sometimes it is difficult to get children to drink milk. Try putting the milk in a glass wi' a straw. Then you can make a pea shooter and fire chewed up bits o' paper across the room!

Blackcurrant

Blackcurrant Ribesnigrum. Common names: Quinsy berries, squinancy berries. Occurrence: a common garden plant throughout Britain, but is only truly native to Yorkshire and the Lake District. It is also found in Europe.
Parts used: the fruit, leaves, bark and root.
Medicinal uses: diuretic, diaphoretic, febrifuge, refrigerant, detergent. The fruit juice is excellent in febrile diseases and can be made to an extract which is good for sore throats. The leaves when infused are cleansing while a root infusion is used in eruptive fevers and has been used to treat cattle. A decoction of the bark is effective against calculus, oedema and haemorrhoids. The fruit was commonly used to make jelly, wine and cheese.
Administered as: juice, infusion or decoction.

Frock Drying

Drying A Cotton Frock

Instead of hanging it over the line with pegs, put a bamboo stick through the sleeves, and with a meat-hook hang it so that the frock is clear of the ground. If the waist is elasticated a small stick about 12 inches long inserted into two old tennis balls will keep the waist extended and stop the seams from dropping.

If it's ane o' Daphne's frocks dry it on the allotment and scare the crows!

Lunchbox Smells

Vinegar gets rid of Lunchbox smells. Soak two bits o' bread in vinegar in the box over night. I did this with Paw's last week and he grabbed it and picked it up on his way to work. He wasn't best pleased at lunch time – but he ate it!

Day To Day Diary

Date _Wallpaper Tips_

Wallpaper

When choosing paper for a room, avoid that which has a variety of colours, or a large showy figure, as furniture can be lost. Large figured papering makes a small room look smaller, but, on the contrary, a paper covered with a small pattern makes a room look larger, and a striped paper, the stripes running from ceiling to floor, makes a low room look higher.

Nae wonder Hen keeps bangin' his heid in the lobby — it's got stripey paper!

Violet

Common names: blue violet, sweet violet, sweet-scented violet.
Occurrence: native to Britain and found widely over Europe, northern Asia and North America.
Parts used: the dried flowers and leaves and whole plant when fresh.
Medicinal uses: antiseptic, expectorant, laxative. The herb is mainly taken as syrup of violets, which has been used to cure the ague, epilepsy, eye inflammation, pleurisy, jaundice and sleeplessness. The flowers possess expectorant properties and have long been used to treat coughs. The flowers may also be crystallized as a sweetmeat or added to salads. The rhizome is strongly emetic and purgative and has violent effects when administered. The seeds also have purgative and diuretic effects and are beneficial in treating urinary complaints. In the early 20th century, violet preparations were thought to be a treatment for cancer. Fresh violet leaves were made into an infusion that was drunk regularly, and a poultice of the leaves was applied to the affected area. The herb was used to allay pain and it is said that it was a particularly good treatment for those suffering from throat cancer. Administered as: infusion, poultice, injection, ointment, syrup and powdered root.

169

Lost corkscrew/Treacle

Housewife's Choice

When The Corkscrew Can't Be Found

Take a wood screw and screw it in, and tie a stout piece of string around the head. Pull straight up but watch and not punch yersel' in the face if it comes oot' wi' a rush.

If the cork crumbles, and you cannae get it oot, then push it in to the bottle. Take care wi' this as you might end up wi' a fountain if you plunge it in too hard. Use a spoon handle to keep it down whilst you decant the precious contents. Strain out the wee bits o' cork.

A Treacle Hint

If you sprinkle flour on your measuring spoon or the dish on the scales before measuring out treacle, you can pour it in

Day To Day Diary

**A stuck lid/
A burned pan**

and then back out without it sticking. When I do this the bairns look that disappointed – there's nae spoon tae lick!

When A Lid Sticks

Here's how to unscrew a tight lid that won't come off : put a rubber band around it to give a good grip and unscrew. If that doesn't work, run the lid under the hot tap to expand it and try again. Nae need tae ask a man – they aye look for some complicated solution such as jammin' the lid in the crack o' a door and usin' it like a vice !

When They've Burned the Bottom o' a Pan

There's nothin' worse. They scrub wi' wire pads an' a'thing. Secret is to put in some biological washin' powder wi' a wee bit water. Leave it aside for a day. The powder eats the burned bits a treat. Rinse tae a sparkle!

171

<u>Vinegar Tips – It's awfy clever stuff –</u>

•<u>Tenderise meat</u> wi' vinegar. An 8 hour soak.

•<u>It kills grass</u> on paths and kills weeds tae,
deter ants wi' it. Make a sprayer.

•<u>It refreshes</u> wilted vegetables. Soak them in
a ½ pint of water and a tbs of vinegar.

•<u>It stops boiled eggs</u> from cracking.
Add 2 tablespoons of vinegar to the water.

•<u>It's a rare cleaner for the fridge.</u>
Use a solution 50/50 water and vinegar.

• <u>Dissolve rust</u> from bolts and other
metals. Soak them in full strength vinegar.

•<u>Relieve itchy, dry skin.</u> Add 2 tablespoons

Day To Day Diary

Date

Vinegar —
Its Many Uses

of vinegar to your bath water.

• Soothe a sore throat. Mix a teaspoon of vinegar in a glass of water. Gargle.

• Get rid of kitchen cooking smells. Simmer a pan of vinegar and water.

• Unclog a steam iron. Pour 50/50 vinegar and water into the iron's water chamber. Turn it on to steam and leave it for 5 minutes upright position. Then unplug and allow to cool. Loose dirt should come out when you empty it.

Cucumber

Cucumber Cucumis sativa. Common name: cowcumber. Occurrence: a native of the East Indies, but was first cultivated in Britain around 1573. Parts used: the whole fruit, peeled or unpeeled, raw and cooked. Medicinal uses: the seeds are diuretic and are an excellent taeniacide and purge. The fruit is very good as a skin cosmetic as it has cooling, healing and soothing effects on irritated skin. Cucumber juice is widely utilised in emollient ointments or creams and is good for sunburn. Administered as: expressed juice, lotion or ointment.

Date <u>Vinegar</u>

Housewife's Choice

•Remove grease from suede. Dip an old toothbrush in vinegar and brush over.

•Rid clothes of smoke smells. Add a cup of vinegar to a steaming bath of hot water. Hang the clothes up.

•Freshen cut flowers. Add 2 tablespoons vinegar and 1 teaspoon sugar to the flower water.

•Soothe stings and sunburn. Lightly dab with vinegar.

BUT MAW, HOW DO YOU GET RID OF THE SMELL OF VINEGAR ?

Baking soda ! It's a natural deodoriser ! It's ca'd Bicarbonate of Soda — and like Vinegar and Lemons it is ane o' these things to hae in your cupboard at a' times. Never be withoot!

174

Day To Day Diary

Date **BICARB**

Baking Soda is a really good friend !
My ain mither used to swear by
bicarbonate of soda. You can use it in
cookin', or in the hame, or even for bee
stings. It's a braw thing to have handy —
and make your scones rise in the oven that
you've just cleaned with it, to get rid of
any smells.

Horace says: "It is a naturally occurring mineral and is
ideal as a cleaning product, as well as a substance to
cook with, and to use as a beauty product. As well as
something you can use to de-pong your fridge.

Cowslip

Primulaveris. Common names:
Herb peter, paigle, peggle, key
flower, key of heaven, fairy
cups, petty mulleins, patsywort,
plumrocks, mayflower, Our Lady's
keys, arthritica.
Occurrence: a common wild
flower in all parts of Great Britain.
Parts used: the flower.

Medicinal uses: sedative,
antispasmodic. It is very good
in relieving restlessness and
insomnia. Commonly brewed
into a wine which was a good
children's medicine in small
doses.
Administered as: an infusion or
wine.

Bicarb

Housewife's Choice

Here are a few things that I use it for:

• _Hair:_ Use a teaspoon o' bicarbonate of soda with your favourite shampoo — the soda removes the build-up of conditioners and hair products and leaves it nice and clean.

• _Laundry:_ For fresh perspiration stains, wet the mark, and then rub in a wee drop bicarbonate of soda before washin' as usual.

• _Cleaning your bathroom._ Mix one cup of bicarbonate of soda with half a cup of vinegar into a paste and use on a cloth to clean grease and marks from your bath, sink and surfaces.

Jacob's ladder

Common names: Greek valerian, charity.
Occurrence: found wild in ditches and streams across England and southern Scotland.
Parts used: the herb.
Medicinal uses: diaphoretic, astringent, alterative, expectorant. A useful drug in fevers and inflammatory diseases, pleurisy, etc. It induces copious perspiration and eases coughs, colds, bronchial and lung complaints.
Administered as: an infusion.

Day To Day Diary

Date **Bicarb**

• Clean your tile groutin: work bicarbonate of soda into the areas you need tae clean.

• Kitchen surfaces: Sprinkle bicarbonate of soda onto a damp cloth and clean stains on kitchen surfaces with it. Your chopping board too!

• Clean your shoes and sandals — many sandals these days are made for walking, and durability, but they can get a wee bit whiffy. Especially Hen's. I think it's because he's that tall that he disnae get a whiff till later than we do. We are closer to the ground. The trick is to mix bicarbonate of soda wi' water to make a paste, and then clean your shoes.

• Windaes — come up a treat with a sprinkle of bicarbonate of soda on a cloth dipped

first in hot water. Rinse your windaes wi'
clean water to get them a' shiny. You can
use vinegar too, as an alternative. Wipe them
after wi' newspaper.

• Carpets — if you have a small accident,
or one of the bairns is sick, sprinkle on
bicarbonate of soda to take out any odour,
and salt to remove the moisture. Repeat as
you need, tae clean.

• Paths — in winter, you can use bicarbonate
of soda as you would use salt to remove ice
and snow from paths in the cauld.

• Brass — mix a paste from a tablespoon of
salt, one tablespoon of bicarbonate of soda and
two tablespoons of flour wi' as much vinegar
as you need. Rub on with a soft cloth. Leave
to dry, and then buff off for a grand shine.

Day To Day Diary

Date <u>Bicarb</u>

• Mop and/or dust rags, to renew and freshen them — I soak these overnight in a bucket of hot water (a quarter of a gallon) with a cup of baking soda and half a cup of salt.

• General purpose cleaner — I mix up two pints of water with four teaspoons of bicarbonate of soda, half a cup of vinegar, and keep it in a spray bottle.

• Bicarbonate of soda is the very dab for getting crayon off a floor. Just use some sprinkled on a cloth and gie it a rub.

Daisy

Common names: bruisewort, bairnwort, eye of the day.
Occurrence: very common all over the British Isles.
Parts used: the root and leaves.
Medicinal uses: it was formerly utilised as a cure for fresh wounds, pains and aches and was taken internally as distilled water to treat fevers and inflammation of the liver.
Administered as: a poultice and distilled water.

<u>Bicarb</u>

• Three-parts bicarbonate of soda to one part-water is a good paste to get rid of grime and grease from the hands. Or replace the water with liquid soap if the stains are ground in.

• All purpose cleaner : I make up an all purpose cleaner that you can use throughout the hoose: mix up two pints of water, four teaspoons of baking soda, half a cup of vinegar and keep this in a spray bottle. Safe to use on countertops, windowsills and even floors. And if the Twins spray each other while my back is turned, I don't need to worry as it's not harmful.

• An open box with an inch of bicarbonate of soda can be left anywhere near smells, to absorb and clear them.

Day To Day Diary

Date **Bicarb**

• You can leave a half cup of baking soda in the toilet overnight to clean it.

• Bicarbonate of soda for dry skin: Mix a cup of oatmeal with a cup of warm water, a tablespoon of vanilla extract and half a cup of baking soda to a smooth paste. Add the mixture to water while you hae a bath. Said to soothe itchy, dry skin.

• A foot bath: add three tablespoons of bicarbonate of soda to a basin of warm water and rest your tootsies. The solution softens skin, removes odour and feels good.

• Stings fae bees, will find instant relief by applying a paste of cold water and bicarbonate of soda tae it for five minutes.

181

<u>Bicarb</u>

Housewife's Choice

• Daphne tried to whiten her <u>teeth</u> with a paste of bicarbonate of soda.

• Granpaw regularly uses a solution of two teaspoons of bicarbonate of soda mixed in a small bowl of warm water for his <u>wallies</u>.

• <u>Prickly heat or poison ivy</u> — we used a paste of bicarbonate of soda and water on a small area of a rash. The water evaporates leaving a white powder. That flakes off if you don't sit still but hopefully by that time, the pain will have died off a wee bit anyway.

<u>Smells</u>

Hen — What's the best way to catch a fish?
– Get Horace tae throw it tae ye!

Fishy Smells :
Cooking fish can be a smelly business but you can get rid o' it. Cut a lemon in half

Day To Day Diary

Date **Bicarb**

and boil it up in a pan with a wee drop water. The steam disperses the aroma and the smell is taken care of.

Pet Accidents

White vinegar mixed in some warm water will help to get rid of the smell left behind by a wee accident.

That Damp Cupboard Smell

Try putting a box with cat litter in it.

We like walnut cake – it's crackin'

Walnut

Common names: carya, Jupiter's nuts, Juglans regia.
Occurrence: cultivated throughout Europe and probably native to Persia.
Parts used: the bark and leaves. The active principle of the walnut tree is nucin or juglon, while the kernels also contain oil, mucilage, albumin, cellulose, mineral matter and water.
Medicinal uses: alterative, laxative, detergent, astringent. The bark and leaves are used in skin problems, e.g. scrofulous diseases, herpes, eczema and for healing indolent ulcers. A strong infusion of the powdered bark has purgative effects, while the walnut has various properties dependent upon its stage of ripeness. Green walnuts are anthelmintic and vermifuge in action and are pickled in vinegar, which is then used as a gargle for sore and ulcerated throats. The wood is used for furniture, gun stocks and for cabinets. Walnut oil expressed from the kernels is used in wood polishing, painting and is used as butter or frying oil.
Administered as: fluid extract, infusion, expressed oil, whole fruit.

The cat litter absorbs the damp smell and leaves it smelling fresh.

Explain that tae a cat!

Microwave Smells

Put a saucer with some lemon juice on it into the microwave. Use full power for two minutes. Then wipe the microwave oven down with a clean cloth.

Plastic Containers

Plastic containers used for picnics and storage can often smell if they are stored empty with their lids on. Put a piece of crumpled up newspaper inside the box, with the lid on and leave overnight. This will take away the smell.

Cigarette Smoke Smell

If you don't like using these overpowering 'freshners' in a car, try soaking two sponges

or absorbent cloths in white vinegar.
Put each into an open container by the
ashtray and another on the back shelf,
overnight – and by the morning all
you'll have to worry about is the smell of
vinegar. Works in a room too if you have
had a smoker to visit.

Garlic
Garlic helps build up your defences against
allergies, and it helps regulate your blood
sugar levels. It's packed wi' vitamins
and nutrients like protein, potassium,
Vitamins A, B, B2 and C, and it's got

Granpaw's no' allowed
his pipe in the hoose. If
he wants a blaw he has
tae stick his heid oot the
windae!

Day To Day Diary

Date

Garlic Is Magic

Calcium and Zinc too! It's a naturally powerful antibiotic that contains sulphur and works against toxic bacteria, viruses, and fungus. It helps your liver clean out all sorts o' toxins – food additives and suchlike. You can cut a piece of garlic and rub it on a spot. You can soak the garlic in milk if you are worried about the smell. The milk doesn't disturb the antiseptic qualities.

This really works a treat – so Maggie tells me!

Drinking lemon juice or eating a few slices of lemon will stop bad garlic breath. Or, if you crush a clove onto a spoon then add a touch o' olive oil and swallow you get all the

Garlic

Garlic Alliumsativum. Common name: Poor man's treacle.
Occurrence: cultivated throughout Europe since antiquity.
Parts used: the bulb.
Medicinal uses: antiseptic, diaphoretic, diuretic, expectorant, stimulant. It may be externally applied as ointment, lotion, antiseptic or as a poultice. Syrup of garlic is very good for asthma, coughs, difficulty in breathing and chronic bronchitis, while fresh juice has been used to ease tubercular consumption. The essential oil is commonly taken as a supplement in the form of gelatine capsules. Several species of wild garlic are utilised for both medicinal and dietary purposes. Administered as: expressed juice, syrup, tincture, essential oil, poultice, lotion and ointment.

187

More About Garlic

HOUSEWIFE'S CHOICE

goodness of raw garlic but none of the garlic breath problems.

Mrs Gow takes garlic pills to help ward off coughs and colds.

At that first sign o' a cold comin' on, chop up 3 or 4 cloves of raw garlic and eat them or use them in a soup.

You can ease toothache wi' garlic — just take a piece o' raw garlic and rub it on the tooth and gums a couple of times a day.

Warts will disappear — crush fresh garlic cloves and rub on.

Garlic is perhaps one of the cleverest foods in the world. Garlic is part of the same family of vegetables which includes onions, chives, leeks and shallots.

In Horace's history book it says the builders of the pyramids ate garlic every day for strength.

Day To Day Diary

Date *Bites and Stings*

Garlic can thin the blood just like aspirin. Foods like garlic and onions are said to help prevent cancer.

Bites and Stings

Jings! We've been roon' the hooses on this subject! When you need to know whit tae dae in a hurry because you've a bairn crying after a sting, the best thing to remember, I think, is:

Nettle

Urticadioica, Urticaurens. Common names: Common nettle, stinging nettle. Occurrence: widely distributed throughout temperate Europe and Asia, Japan, South Africa and Australia. Parts used: the whole herb, which contains formic acid, mucilage, mineral salts, ammonia and carbonic acid. Medicinal uses: astringent, stimulating, diuretic, tonic. The herb is anti-asthmatic and the juice of the nettle will relieve bronchial and asthmatic troubles, as will the dried leaves when burnt and inhaled. The seeds are taken as an infusion or in wine to ease consumption or ague. Nettles are used widely as a food source and can be made into soup, puddings, tea, beer, juice and used as a vegetable. A hair tonic or lotion can also be made from the nettle. In the Highlands of Scotland, they were chopped, added to egg white and applied to the temples as a cure for insomnia.
Administered as: expressed juice, infusion, decoction, seeds, dried herb, dietary item.

Bites and Stings

Housewife's Choice

Bicarb for bee stings and vinegar for wasps. There's folk that say that that nane o' the auld remedies actually help that much, but I've seen such misery o'er the years that when we afternoon tea ladies sat and had a blether I think it's fair tae say that we had mair suggestions aboot this than a'thing else!

Let's try and sort it oot! Wasps, Hornets, Bees and Ants are venomous. Mosquitoes, Sand Flies, Bugs and Ticks are non-venomous but effects can still be serious — for example you can get Lyme Disease from ticks.

The difference is aboot the kind o' the bite or sting. Venomous insects attack as their kind o' defence and they inject a painful, toxic venom wi' their stings.

Bee stings

Non-venomous insects bite so that they can hae a right good feed on your blood! You do get irritation and allergic reactions from non-venomous bites, but the severe reactions such as anaphylactic shock only happen fae venomous stings.

When bees sting, they leave their sting and their venom sach attached. Venom continues to pump in through their stinger until their venom sach is empty or the sting is taken oot.

Bees die after they sting. Wasps and hornets don't leave their stings behind and so can sting you o'er and o'er again!

When you are stung by a bee, get the sting out because the longer it stays in the wound, the deeper it will pierce and emit more of the poison, which is the cause of the pain and inflammation.

Day To Day Diary

Date <u>Insect Bites</u>

The pulling out of the sting should be done carefully, and wi' a steady hand, to avoid breaking it. When the sting is extracted, suck the wounded part, if possible, and hopefully very little inflammation, if any, will follow. If in doubt get medical help.

To Remove a Sting — pit the edge o' a table knife against the skin, next to where the sting is. Press doon, and wipe the knife across the skin surface and the

Dandelion

Dandelion Taraxacumofficinale.
Common names: priest's crown, swine's snout.
Occurrence: widely found across the northern temperate zone in pastures, meadows and waste ground.
Parts used: the root and leaves. The main constituents of the root are taraxacin, a bitter substance, and taraxacerin, an acid resin, along with the sugar inulin.
Medicinal uses: diuretic, tonic and slightly aperient. It acts as a general body stimulant, but chiefly acts on the liver and kidneys. Dandelion is used as a bitter tonic in atonic dyspepsia as a mild laxative and to promote increased appetite and digestion. The herb is best used in combination with other herbs and is used in many patent medicines. Roasted dandelion root is also used as a coffee substitute and helps ease dyspepsia, gout and rheumatism. Administered as: fluid and solid extract, decoction, infusion and tincture.

Simple Remedies

stinger. This removes the stinger without it injecting more venom, which is what happens when you remove the stinger wi' tweezers or wi' your fingers.

Other remedies for insect bites that we collected:

• Mix 1 tsp. lavender essential oil with 1 tbsp. vegetable oil. Mix the ingredients and apply to the bite, except around eyes.

• A sting poultice can be made like this:
1 tbsp. echinacea root tincture.
1 tbsp. distilled water.
⅛ tsp. lavender essential oil.
1 tbsp. bentonite clay.
Mix the echinacea, water and lavender.
Add the liquid slowly to the clay while stirring. Once mixed, the resulting paste should stick to the skin.
Apply on the injured area. Store the

WHY DO BEES HUM?
COS THEY DON'T KNOW THE WORDS

194

Day To Day Diary

Date **Auld soothers for Bites**

poultice in a tight lid container. If it does dry out add water until moistened enough to stick to the skin.

• Onion – a slice of raw onion placed on an insect bite will discourage infection and draw the poison out.

Auld 'soothers' for Insect Bites – One raw egg, well beaten, half a pint of vinegar, one ounce of spirits of turpentine, a quarter of an ounce of spirits of wine, a quarter of an ounce of camphor. These ingredients to be beaten well together, then put in a bottle and shaken for ten minutes, after which, to

Nettle Stings

A nettle sting can be cured by rubbing the part with rosemary, mint, or sage leaves.

Dock leaves bruised, and rubbed on are a remedy, and the great thing is that they can usually be found where nettles grow.

Midge Bites

be corked down tightly to exclude the air.
In half an hour it is ready for use. Rub in,
two, three, or four times a day.

Midge Bites.

Granpaw says The Highland Fling came aboot because o' midges gettin' in aboot the kilt!

Dissolve one ounce of bicarbonate of soda
in a pint of hot water. Soak in and wring
out a large piece of cotton wool and apply to
the bitten part. Bandage over, and repeat in
two hours. Do not scratch the bitten parts.

Garlic — One of the quickest and easiest
remedies for those terrible mosquito bites is
a simple clove of garlic. Cut a clove in half
and rub it right onto the bite.

Preventive Measures can be taken against
Mosquito Bites. — Dissolve one teaspoonful
of eucalyptus oil in two ounces of rectified
spirit (60 percent.). Use as a spray over

Day To Day Diary

Date <u>Repellent</u>

stockings and any bare parts, i.e. wrists and neck, before entering woods or fields or any other place where midges are found. Mrs Gow gets stuff from the Avon lady called "Skin So Soft" that is the very dab as a midge repellent.

<u>Another Insect Repellent</u> — make a mixture of <u>Citronella Oil</u> and <u>Lemon Grass Oil</u> mixed with Sweet Almond Oil at a ratio of 10 drops each of the Citronella and Lemon Grass Oil mixed with about ½ a teaspoon of the Sweet Almond Carrier Oil. This mixture has a pleasant smell to it so is not as bad as some of the "Insect Repellents" which are available on the market.

<u>Jellyfish</u> — Just as wasps and bees can be a right nuisance at family picnics.

Jellyfish can be a major problem on days oot at the beach. Try to check the water before entering. But, if you do get stung, standard advice is to try and rinse the jellyfish tentacles off in hot water – as hot as the patient can stand –but work up to the heat and take care not to scald the stung person. The venom is protein based, so if you 'cook' it, it stops working. If there is no hot water immediately available use salt not fresh water. Fresh water will make the sting more painful. Remove any remaining tentacles with a stick, gloved hand, shell or tweezers. Don't let the tentacles touch you or your clothing.

• Some folk say that for a box jellyfish sting you can try cider vinegar or white vinegar.

• It is always best to put something on

Day To Day Diary

to cover bites or stings when bairns are suffering. There is always a danger of the bite becoming infected because of scratching.

Ticks & Mites — Travellers moving through dense undergrowth or exploring caves may find ticks or mites attached to their skin. Any stage of the life of a tick can transmit disease — including the larva which is the size of a speck of soot.

If you are bitten by a tick never try and twist it oot!

Don't use yer bare hands to remove the tick. Never touch a tick with bare skin or yer fingernails. The latex gloves you should have in your first aid kit are best but, at a push, shield yer fingers with tissue or paper. To remove a tick you are trying to remove it in

Horace says : Ticks and mites are actually arachnids and not insects!

<u>Ticks And Mites</u>

Housewife's Choice

its entirety and to prevent it releasing its stomach contents into your bite wound or any open skin. The best thing is a proper tick tool. Alternatives are tweezers (cleaned before and after removing each tick) or a length of thread wrapped around the ticks mouthparts at the skin. (Do not squeeze or crush the tick's body, do not try to burn it off or apply petroleum jelly or stuff like that. Pull gently and steadily without twisting. Keep the tick in an airtight jar or poly bag and freeze it when you get home wi' a note o' the date, so if you do feel ill, you can take it to the doctor with you (this can help diagnosis). Clean the skin wound afterwards and your hands and any equipment you used.

* Remember — ticks can carry Lyme Disease. See a doctor if you feel poorly if you've had tick bites *

Day To Day Diary

Date **Tea Tree Oil**

The Good Neighbour

Tea Tree Oil

Tea Tree oil is an essential oil obtained by the steam distillation of leaves of a plant native to Australia called Melaleuca alternifolia. In years gone by, the leaves were used as a tea-substitute, which is why Tea Tree oil is so called. The part used in medicine is the oil taken from the leaves. Australian aboriginals used tea tree leaves by crushing the leaves for healing skin cuts, burns, and infections and applying them to the affected area. Tea Tree oil contains terpenoids, which have antiseptic and antifungal properties.

Tea Tree oil is used for the following conditions:
• Acne and skin problems
• Athlete's foot
• Dandruff
• Tea Tree is one of only two essential oils (Lavender is the other) which is used neat on the skin by applying one or two drops directly to spots, cuts, insect bites, stings, blisters, warts, verrucas, cold sores, shingles and Chickenpox lesions.
• Combined with Eucalyptus or Peppermint oils Tea Tree, in a steam inhalation bath can be an effective

Tea tree oil - versatile.

method of clearing the airways of cattarh. Add 3 drops to a bowl of boiling water, cover your head with a towel and inhale the steam deeply for several minutes.
• As a mouthwash - dilute 3 drops of Tea Tree in a teaspoon of brandy. Stir into a glass of warm water and gargle. (Don't swallow).
• Chewing gum can be removed from hair or clothing by applying neat Tea Tree oil.

Mrs Gow swears by Tee Tree Oil for skin complaints and it is marvellous stuff. I found this wee cutting in the papers.

Quick Tips

HINTS TO HELP
with
Home-making
Sewing
Knitting
Cooking
Baking

Presented with "People's Friend"

IT is with great pleasure we present this Book to our readers, a gift we hope will prove a lasting boon in the household.

The hints cover a wide field—homely measures to adopt when emergency arises, the care of your furnishings, time-saving tips to follow in cooking, sewing, knitting, and so on.

The Book comes with the very best wishes of the "People's Friend" staff.

The Editor

Home Truths

BOTTLES.—To prevent the labels on bottles from coming off or being stained, paint over them with clear nail varnish.

Clean narrow-necked bottles by putting in some crushed egg shells and swilling round with hot water.

BOTTLE TOPS.—When taking the cap off a bottle which you wish to reseal, place a coin on top of the cap first. This prevents the cap being dented and enables you to reseal the bottle, making it airtight.

CLEANING.—When cleaning out rooms, pin a paper bag to your apron. Ashtrays and rubbish can be emptied into this as you work, and then the bag and its contents can be thrown away.

CLOCK.—Keep your kitchen clock in a Polythene bag to protect it from dampness and steam.

COATHANGERS.—To keep the collars of garments from being creased at the back, unscrew the hook of the coathanger. Slip on an empty reel and screw back in place.

It's a good idea to wrap rubber bands round the ends of unpadded hangers. Dresses and other clothes won't slip off easily.

COMBS.—If the teeth of a new comb are too sharp, draw along the striking side of a matchbox two or three times.

CORKS.—If a cork is too big for a bottle, cut a wedge from the centre instead of paring the sides.

Before inserting a cork in a bottle, stretch a few inches of tape across the top of the bottle, then press in the cork. To remove, simply pull ends of tape.

Small corks in little bottles may break when you try to pull them out with a full-sized corkscrew. Try using a cup hook instead.

CUSHIONS.—Before filling with feathers, rub the inside of the lining with hard soap to make it more difficult for the feathers to get through.

To refluff feather cushions which have lost their softness, open up one of the seams, insert a bicycle pump and pump air into the cushions. This will plump up the feathers.

CUTLERY.—When polishing cutlery, use a pipe-cleaner for getting between the prongs of the fork.

Remove any "fishy" smell from cutlery by rubbing with a piece of lemon after articles have been washed.

CUT GLASS.—Use a small nailbrush to remove dirt from the crevices, then rinse in warm water, drain and dry. Never use too hot water.

Pick up the tiny fragments of broken glass with a cake of kitchen soap. Then cut off the slice of soap containing the glass and throw it away.

ELECTRIC BULBS.—Clean with methylated spirits instead of water. There is then no danger of dampness getting into the fixtures, as the spirits evaporate quickly.

FLOOR POLISH.—Apply with old newspaper, as this does not soak up the polish and can be burnt afterwards.

(Continued on back page)

CONTENTS

On The Spot

BALL-POINT PEN.—Stains on fingers can be lifted with nail varnish remover. Apply with cotton wool.

BLOOD STAINS.—Soak fabric and wash immediately in cold water to which salt has been added. Never boil before removing stain.

CHOCOLATE.—Soak stain in strong borax water for half an hour. Pour boiling water through and wash in the usual way.

COD LIVER OIL.—Remove with benzol or petrol. Wash thoroughly with warm, soapy water.

COFFEE.—Mix ½ oz. borax in ½ pint warm water. Sponge stain well with this solution, then rinse with clear water. Repeat as many times as necessary.

FRUIT STAINS.—Fresh stains can be removed from linen by pouring boiling water through from a height. Obstinate stains should be rubbed with glycerine and allowed to stand for one hour before having this treatment.

GRASS.—On white clothes, sponge stains with a solution of ammonia and water. On coloured materials, moisten stain well with paraffin or glycerine, leave for an hour, then rinse in warm water.

GREASE.—To treat blankets for grease stains, rub glycerine thickly over the spots. Leave for an hour, then sponge with ammonia and water. Make a ring of powdered magnesia round the stain to prevent the glycerine from spreading.

INK.—To remove from delicate or coloured fabrics, cover immediately with salt. Rinse when all the ink has been absorbed, then wash as usual.

LACQUER PAINT.—Soak stain in a little methylated spirits for a few minutes and rub. When stain is removed, rub dry with a cloth.

LIPSTICK.—First rub stain with petroleum jelly, then wash in hot, soapy water. If this fails, try rubbing the stain with hydrogen peroxide.

MEAT JUICE.—Soak stain in cold water for a short time, then wash in usual way.

MILDEW.—Remove by soaking stains overnight in sour milk, and dry in the sun without rinsing. Repeat several times if necessary.

OIL.—Treat by putting a few drops of turpentine on a soft cloth and rub gently over the mark.

PERFUME.—Remove stains from polished furniture by rubbing very lightly and quickly with methylated spirits, finishing with plenty of linseed oil.

RUST.—To remove from material, chop up some rhubarb and boil in a little water until reduced by half. Using this solution, boil the stained article for quarter of an hour.

SAUCEPANS.—Of aluminium or enamel if badly stained can be cleaned by rubbing with a cork dipped in damp salt.

SEA-WATER.—Remove from shoes by rubbing with milk and allowing it to dry in. Then wash with a detergent solution and dab the shoes dry. Polish in usual way.

SCORCHED LINEN.—Rub scorch with a piece of raw onion and leave for a short time. Then soak in cold water and mark will fade.

STAINS.—When removing stains from clothes always put a piece of clean blotting paper under the material. It absorbs dirt and superfluous liquid.

Another hint, when removing a stain with water or spirit cleaner, *stretch* the fabric over an embroidery hoop before starting.

TEA STAINS.—If obstinate, dilute one part glycerine in two parts water and apply to stain. Leave for a short time and wash in usual way.

Above—To treat grease stains on delicate fabrics, lay garment on blotting paper and hold a heated poker just above the surface. Renew blotting paper as this becomes soiled.

Right—Boiling water poured from a height will help remove fruit stains from linen.

3

Under Your Feet

CARPETS.—To remove pressure marks from a carpet, hold a steam or ordinary iron over the mark, then brush lightly.

CARPETS.—To pick up threads from a carpet easily, whisk a damp scrubbing brush over the surface.

FRAYED CARPETS.—Cut away frayed edges and bind with iron-on adhesive carpet binding.

PATCHING CARPETS.—Cut out worn part neatly with a razor blade. Cut patch from new carpeting to fit. Paste raw edges with adhesive to prevent fraying. Stick piece of hessian, half inch larger than patch, on to backing. Paste hessian with adhesive, insert patch, and hammer down.

TO REVIVE COLOUR.—Sponge carpet or rug with water to which a few drops of ammonia have been added.

CORK FLOORING.—To keep in good condition, treat with a plastic seal as soon as it is laid. Polish with plastic emulsion. Clean with a damp mop, finishing off with a dry cloth daily. Stubborn marks can be removed with fine steel wool.

FLOOR BOARDS.—Gaps can be filled with papier mache made by soaking old newspapers

PAPER WORK

BUYING WALLPAPER.—It is useful to know that a roll is approximately 21 inches wide and 34½ feet long. It will cover an area of about 7 square yards (63 square feet).

WALLPAPER PASTE.—A standard 2 oz. packet of cellulose adhesive will make a gallon of paste—enough for about five rolls of wallpaper.

TO CLEAN WALLPAPER.—Freshen dingy wallpaper in this way : Dissolve two tablespoonfuls of washing soda in one cupful warm water and stir in enough flour to make a very stiff dough. With a piece of dough the size of the hand, work across one breadth of pattern, turning and kneading the dough so that there is always a fresh surface against the paper.

TO PATCH WALLPAPER.—Mark a rough outline of the required patch on the paper to be used. Tear round the outline of the patch. Smooth down edges with sandpaper on the reverse side. Stick the patch in place and smooth down with a soft cloth.

TO REMOVE WALLPAPER.—Use whitewash brush to soak wall with boiling water. Leave till well loosened, then tear off paper from lower edge upwards. Scrape off remainder with broad-bladed putty knife, being careful not to injure plaster.

GREASE SPOTS ON WALLPAPER.—Place a piece of blotting paper over the spots and press with a warm iron, changing the blotting paper as it absorbs the grease.

4

shredded small in a weak solution of size. Press between floor boards and level off, allowing to harden before rubbing down with coarse sandpaper.

LINO.—Avoid washing and scrubbing as far as possible. A cloth dipped in paraffin will remove dirt, and obstinate marks can be removed with fine steel wool dipped in turpentine.

LINO.—To deal with raised lino, cut a slit in the bulge, letting the cut follow the pattern. Spread linoleum cement under the slit on each side, working the cement well underneath the edges. Press down firmly and wipe away any smears from the surface at once.

RUBBER FLOORING.—Wash only very occasionally, using soapy water or a mild soapless detergent. Avoid scrubbing or harsh cleansers. Polish sparingly with plastic emulsion, allowing this to dry for half an hour. For daily care, dust with a dry mop.

THERMOPLASTIC TILES.—When cleaning, avoid the use of strong detergents, paraffin, turpentine or paste wax polishes. Remove marks with a cloth well wrung out in mild soapless detergent suds. For really stubborn marks, use a pad of steel wool dipped in the same suds. Polish regularly with plastic emulsion.

WOODEN FLOORS.—Do not wash unless the surface has been properly treated with a floor seal. Wax polish sparingly and not too often. Buff to a high shine and dry-mop daily.

Ink spilt on a carpet should be covered immediately with salt, and the salt renewed as it absorbs the ink.

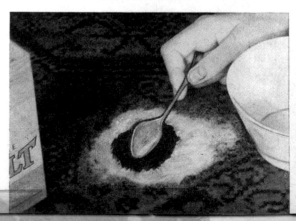

Furbish For Furniture

a cloth well wrung out in hot detergent suds. Rinse with a clean, damp cloth, then wipe dry with chamois leather.

CARVED WOOD.—Use a clear liquid polish for intricate carving. Apply with a soft cloth, then buff with a clean, soft brush.

CELLULOSE FINISH.—Furniture with cellulosed finish should be wiped with a damp chamois leather. Do not apply polish.

CHAIR LEGS.—To prevent marking the floor, glue small rounds of felt to the base of each leg.

CUPBOARD DOORS.—Should these stick, remove any dust from the runners of the door, apply furniture polish to the runners and polish well.

CURTAIN RINGS.—Paint curtain rings and hooks with clear nail varnish. This will protect them from rust.

Slip a thimble over the end of a curtain rod when slipping it through curtains to avoid catching.

DARKENED FURNITURE.—To revive rub over with a soft cloth moistened with white spirit (turpentine substitute). If the furniture is sticky and retains fingermarks, wash with warm soapy water, rinse with several changes of clear, warm water and dry thoroughly with a soft cloth.

DENTS.—When on a wooden surface moisten the dent with warm water, allow to soak in for a few minutes then wipe dry. Cover dent and surrounding area with a double thickness of blotting paper and apply a warm—not hot—iron to the paper. Several applications may be necessary.

DOORSTOPS.—Fasten an old cotton reel to the floor with a long screw down the middle hole and paint or stain to match the floor.

DRAWERS.—If a drawer sticks, take it out and rub all working edges with candlewax or lead pencil. Run drawer backwards and forwards, renewing wax or pencil until movement is smooth.

Line drawers used for cosmetics with blotting paper so that any spilt liquid will be soaked up and will not mark the wood.

FELT.—Glue odd pieces of felt to vases and ashtrays to prevent them marking polished furniture.

HOT FAT.—When spilt on wood, cover with salt immediately. This will soak up fat and prevent it marking the wood.

LEATHER.—Dust leather furniture daily and polish occasionally with a little good quality shoe or leather cream. About once a year, treat specially by sponging with a solution of four teaspoonfuls vinegar and a teaspoonful of ammonia to two pints of cold water. Rub dry, then to feed leather, work a little castor oil into it with your fingers or a piece of clean flannel. Leave to dry, then polish.

PAINTED FURNITURE. — Remove fingermarks with a clean cloth sprinkled with a few drops of paraffin, then wipe with a cloth dipped in very hot water.

REXINE.—Clean Rexine-covered furniture with

SCRATCHES.—Rub scratches on polished wood gently in the direction of the grain with fine wire wool saturated in pure turpentine. Polish afterwards with wax polish in the usual way.

UPHOLSTERY.—To mend a tear slip a piece of self-adhesive two-inch binding under tear and press raw edges over it. Or a blanket-stitch join can be used. Blanket-stitch each side of tear, then catch sides together. Use strong thread—buttonhole twist or carpet thread for preference.

WHITE MARKS ON WOOD.—Marks from hot dishes or spilled water will often go if cigarette ash is sprinkled over the mark and surrounding area. Dampen a clean cloth with vinegar and rub the ashy surface, always rubbing lightly in the same direction as the grain of the wood.

BRUSH WORK

BROOMS AND BRUSHES.—Remove fluff from brushes with an old comb. This saves washing over frequently.

HAIR BRUSHES.—Wash in warm soapy water, then rinse thoroughly to remove all traces of soap. Stiffen bristles by rinsing in water to which salt has been added.

PAINT BRUSHES.—Wash immediately after use with soap and warm water. Rinse in clear water and shape by pulling through the hands. Place in a jar to dry with the handles downwards.

EMULSION PAINT.—Remove from brushes before it is quite dry with methylated spirit, cleaning fluid or brush cleaner. Follow with thorough wash in soap and water.

OIL PAINT.—Clean from brushes while wet with ordinary paraffin.

PAINTING.—Prevent paint from running down your paint brush by wrapping a gauze bandage round the middle of the brush. Anchor the gauze with a rubber band.

PAINTING.—Slip a rubber band over the bristles of your paint brush when doing a job that calls for more than usual neatness. This binds the bristles together and gives them clean lines.

PAINT TINS.—Knock the lids on tightly and store upside down to prevent a skin forming. Turn right side up about ten minutes before using.

SHOE BRUSHES.—To clean, soak in turpentine, then wash in hot soapy water to which ammonia has been added. Rinse in warm water, adding one teaspoonful ammonia to one pint of water.

VARNISH.—Put the can in a bowl of hot water. This thins down the varnish and makes the job much easier.

5

Cookery Nook

BATTER FOR FISH.—When mixing batter, add a tablespoonful of vinegar to the mixture. The batter will stick more closely to the fish. There is no taste of vinegar.

BISCUITS.—Keep fresh by putting in a Polythene bag before putting them away in a tin.

A few cubes of sugar in the bottom of the tin will also help.

BUTTER.—When measuring for baking, cut butter and fat diagonally from corner to corner. This gives a more accurate measure.

CAKE MIXING.—When creaming cake mixtures you'll find it easier if you place a damp cloth under the bowl. This prevents bowl sliding about.

CAKE MIXTURE.—To prevent cake mixture sticking to the wooden spoon it's a good idea to first rub the spoon well with greased paper.

Before putting cake mixture into cases, dip the spoon in hot water and the mixture will drop off easily.

CAKE TINS.—Before storing cakes, line tin with blotting paper to absorb moisture. This will keep the food fresh and the tins rust-free.

CHOPS AND STEAK.—When frying, insert the fork in the fat to turn instead of in the meat. This will prevent the juices from running.

COOKERY BOOK.—Keep clean while cooking by slipping a Polythene bag over the page you are using. This will also keep the book open at the right place.

EGGS.—Before breaking eggs for poaching or frying, put them in boiling water for half a minute to prevent the white from spreading in the pan.

A cracked egg can still be boiled by rubbing over the crack with dripping before putting the egg in water.

FANCY CAKES.—To store, place a teacup in the middle of the tin, place the cakes round it, rest a plate on top of the cup and fill the second layer with more cakes.

FLANS.—Before making a flan cut two strips of greaseproof paper and lay them across the tin in the shape of a cross. Leave the ends projecting above the top. When cooked, the flan can be lifted out by the paper strips without breaking.

FISH.—To keep fresh in warm weather, lay on a plate, cover with greaseproof paper and sprinkle the paper with cooking salt.

FRIED FISH.—To prevent fish sticking to the pan, sprinkle a little salt in the pan before putting in the fat.

FROSTING.—Dip the rims of the glasses to be frosted for party drinks in lemon juice, then in sugar and leave to set.

GLASS JARS.—To prevent from cracking when hot jam or jelly is poured in, stand a wooden fork or spoon in the jar.

HARD-BOILED EGGS.—Put in cold water for a few minutes, then tap the shell all over with a knife. The shell will then come off all in one piece.

HOT DISHES.—To remove hot dishes from the oven, place them on a meat tin or baking sheet to provide a better hold.

JAM-MAKING.—Screw a cup hook into the top of the wooden spoon you are using. It can then be hung on the edge of the pan between stirrings.

Scum can be prevented by dropping a piece of butter into the pan when it is boiling. Never skim jam too soon as it is only froth which rises at first.

JAM POT COVERS.—If these become glued together, lay a thin paper over them and press with a warm iron.

Left—Cut a large fruit cake in the middle and take slices from the centre, then push halves together again to keep moist and in good condition.

Above—Place two strips of greaseproof paper crosswise in the tin before baking a flan. When ready, the flan can be lifted out easily by the projecting ends of the paper.

6

and *Kitchen Shortcuts*

LEMONS.—Before grating, run the grater under the cold water tap and the gratings will slip off easily.

When you require only a few drops of lemon juice, prick one end of the lemon with a fork and squeeze out a little juice. The opening will close again and the lemon will stay fresh.

LETTUCE.—Keep fresh by placing in a dry saucepan and covering with a close-fitting lid.

MILK.—To prevent from boiling over, rinse a pottery egg-cup in cold water, then place it upside down in a pan. Pour in the milk and boil as usual.

MUSTARD.—Add a pinch of salt when mixing to prevent it from turning hard.

NEW CAKE.—When cutting, divide into two. Cut required amount from one half and close up again. This keeps the cake from becoming dry.

OMELETTES.—Add a dessertspoonful of cold water to the beaten egg to make the omelette lighter.

ONIONS.—To fry quickly, place in a pan with just enough water to cover, boil for five minutes, then strain and fry in the usual way.

PACKETS.—Once a packet has been opened, seal the top with adhesive tape to prevent spilling and to keep the contents fresh.

PASTRY.—To roll rich pastry such as shortcake, place the mixture on a lightly-floured board and cover with a piece of greased greaseproof paper. Roll out in the usual way.

PEEL.—If you require orange or lemon rind for use in cakes or puddings, remove it with a potato peeler. You'll find the peel is just the right thickness.

PICNIC FOOD.—Wrap in aluminium foil as this deflects the sun's rays and keeps the food crisp and fresh.

POTATOES.—When roasting or baking, remove the centre with an apple corer and they will be cooked in half the time.

ROYAL ICING.—Before using, add a few drops of glycerine to stop the icing from turning rock hard.

SALT CELLARS.—Put a few grains of rice inside to keep the salt from caking.

SAUCEPANS.—The top part of a glass fireproof casserole makes an excellent lid for a saucepan. You can see at a glance if the contents are boiling too quickly.

SAUSAGES.—Before frying, dip in hot water and prick with a fork. This prevents them bursting while cooking.

SILVER BALLS.—When decorating a cake use small eyebrow tweezers to place silver balls on the icing.

SOUP.—If soup has been over-salted, add a raw potato or a little coarse sugar to remove the taste of the salt.

STALE BREAD.—Wrap in a cloth dipped in hot water. When the crust feels moist and soft, place in a moderate oven until crisp again.

STEWED FRUIT.—Less sugar is required if a pinch of baking soda is added shortly before fruit is sufficiently cooked.

SUGAR.—If you run out of castor sugar while baking, roll out some ordinary sugar with a rolling pin and use instead.

SYRUP.—When weighing syrup, place the tin on the scales and take out spoonfuls until the weight has dropped by the required amount.

TOMATOES.—Place in boiling water for a few minutes and the skin will come off easily.

Before frying, dip the tomato slices in vinegar. This helps to keep them whole.

If tomatoes have gone soft, make firm again by putting in cold water to which a little salt has been added.

Above—Biscuits keep crisp if a cube or two of sugar is stored in the tin with them.

Right—When cooking sausages, you'll find sugar tongs ideal for turning and lifting them.

Wash-Day Wisdom

ANGORA WOOL.—When ironing angora or brushed wool the iron should be held just clear of the damp pressing cloth and should not rest on the garment.

BLOUSES.—When washing silk or nylon blouses add two lumps of sugar to the rinsing water. This gives them the right amount of stiffness if they are ironed when still quite damp.

COLLARS.—If collars are too dry for ironing, hold them in the steam of a boiling kettle for a few minutes. This dampens them evenly and just enough.

COLOUR FASTNESS.—To test a patterned fabric, wash a small sample in warm soapsuds and iron while still damp over a white cloth. If the colour comes out on the cloth the garment should be dry-cleaned.

To remove starch from iron, treat with bicarbonate of soda.

DAMPENING CLOTHES.—An old talcum powder container filled with water is useful for dampening clothes before ironing.

Or dampen garments with a wet sponge. It holds quite a lot of water and dampens evenly.

DETERGENT POWDERS.—Pierce a hole in the packet with a thick knitting needle instead of using the " press to open " tag. You'll save waste.

FABRIC GLOVES. — After washing light-coloured fabric gloves add a little starch to the rinsing water. It gives renewed crispness and the gloves don't get soiled so quickly.

GLOVES.—When drying chamois or leather gloves use the handle of a wooden spoon as a finger stretcher.

IRONS.—To remove starch, wait till the iron is cool, then rub with a damp cloth sprinkled with baking soda. Wipe off with a clean damp cloth and run iron over waxed paper.

IRONING.—Keep clothes damp by putting into a Polythene bag until you are ready to iron them.

8

LACY WOOL GARMENTS.—When washing, put into an old pillow-slip to prevent splitting the threads. After rinsing, roll in a thick towel to remove moisture. Dry flat and press lightly with a warm iron over a damp cloth.

NYLON GARMENTS.—When washing, scrub grubby parts with a nailbrush dipped in dry soap flakes. Otherwise handle as gently as possible.

NYLON STOCKINGS.—When drying outside, drop a penny inside the toe to prevent them twisting round the line.

NYLON UNDIES.—If these have become dingy, soak overnight in a solution of very hot water and borax. Next day rinse in hot water.

SOCKS.—To prevent shrinking, cut pieces of stiff cardboard a little larger than the sole of the foot, and place inside each newly washed sock. Hang up by the toes to dry.

WOOLLENS.—When washing for the first time, add a teaspoonful of glycerine to the final rinsing water to help prevent shrinking or stretching.

ON YOUR METAL

ALUMINIUM PANS.—Do not try to remove burnt-on food with a knife. Soak in water overnight. If burn is obstinate, rub with fine steel wool and soap. Get rid of black marks by putting vinegar in the boiling water when using pan for steaming.

BAKING TRAYS.—Season new trays by greasing inside and out with lard. Put in the oven till lard has melted and wash in warm, soapy water.

BRASS.—After cleaning, a final rub with a liquid silicone furniture cream will help preserve the shine.

CHROMIUM PLATE.—Dust and rub regularly with a soft cloth. If badly stained, wash in warm soapy water, dry and rub with a soft cloth. Rust marks can be removed with chrome cleaner.

COPPER.—Use an impregnated cloth or metal polish regularly, finishing off with liquid silicone furniture polish. Wash dull copper in warm water before polishing. Verdigris can be removed with a cut lemon dipped in salt, or a little vinegar and salt.

FRYING PAN.—Before using a new pan, wash thoroughly and sprinkle with enough salt to cover the base. Heat gently until salt becomes warm. Tip out salt and rub pan with kitchen paper. Now melt a small piece of lard in the pan until it is really hot, tip out, and rub round with kitchen paper.

KETTLES.—To keep " fur " to a minimum, once a week fill the kettle with water and boil with a tablespoonful of vinegar.

PEWTER.—Stubborn tarnish and old polish can be removed with a good brass polish followed by pewter polish.

STOVE TOPS.—Burnt-on food can be removed with fine steel wool and soap. Make sure hot plate taps are off and the hot plate is cool before cleaning.

TARNISHED SILVER.—Clean with plate powder or tarnish removing solution. Once it is clean, a daily rub with an impregnated cloth is all it should require.

Knit-Wit

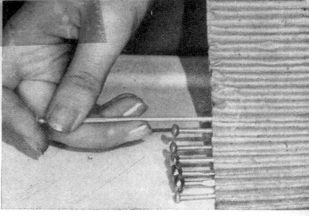

BUTTONS.—Choose buttons suited to the style and thickness of the wool. Buttons which are too large or too heavy for the buttonholes may stretch the fabric permanently.

CASTING-OFF.—When a cast-off edge must stretch, as in a pullover with no neck opening, use a knitting needle one size larger in the right hand. If a tight edge is required, use a needle one size smaller.

ELBOWS.—When elbows wear thin, unpick the sleeves out of the armholes and stitch into the opposite armhole. This brings the worn part to the top and away from the elbow.

JERSEY SLEEVES.—Work sleeves for a child's jersey from shoulder to cuff so that if the elbows wear through the sleeve can be pulled down from the cuff and a new piece knitted on. If working from directions which start at the cuff, proceed as follows:—Cast on the number cast off, increase at top instead of decreasing, and decrease below armholes instead of increasing, knitting the cuff last.

TO LENGTHEN A JUMPER.—Knit the extra rows required after the side decreasings are finished and before starting the armhole shapings. Lengthen sleeves by knitting extra between the last sleeve increases and the beginning of top shaping.

MACHINE STITCHING.—Instead of back-stitching seam by hand, machine with silk or cotton about a quarter of an inch from the edge, taking care that fabric is not pulled or dragged.

NEEDLE NUMBERS.—If you have difficulty in reading the size numbers on your knitting needles, rub a little powder over them and even the faintest numbers will show up more clearly.

PATTERN ADJUSTMENT.—If your pattern is on the small side it will knit up approximately 2 inches wider if needles one size larger are used. It will be 2 inches less in width if needles one size smaller are used.

PINNING OUT.—Pin a checked towel to the ironing cloth before pinning out the knitting and the lines on the towel will act as a guide.

PRESSING.—Place each piece separately on an ironing blanket, right side down, and pin out to

A piece of cartridge paper makes an ideal holder for knitting needles.

measurements given in pattern. Press under a damp cloth with a hot iron. Do not run iron backwards and forwards, but press one part, lift iron, press it down on next part, and so on. Avoid pressing ribbed edges.

ROW MARKER.—If you want to mark a certain row in your knitting, snap a press stud at the end.

SEAM FOR LACE.—Use back-stitch for a seam in a lace pattern where the edge may be uneven. With right sides together, work a row of back-stitch about a quarter of an inch from the edge. Do not pull wool too tightly.

SETTING IN SLEEVES.—Pin into place on the wrong side, easing on the top if sleeves are too full. Always press carefully to avoid stretching.

SHOULDER SEAM.—Overheading worked on the right side gives a neat effect. The shoulder edges are placed together, wrong sides meeting. Now overhead, being careful to pick up the outer edge of the loops of the cast-off chain edge each time.

SLEEVES.—Cast on and work both sleeves at the same time, using a separate ball of wool for each sleeve. In this way the decreases are worked on the same rows and the sleeves are exactly the same length.

STITCH HOLDING.—Before slipping stitches on to a safety-pin, put a small button on the pin to prevent the stitches from tangling round the hinge.

TENSION.—Before you start to knit a garment, cast on about 20 st. using needles and wool indicated, and work about 2 inches in the stitch used. Press, then measure. If you have more stitches and rows to the inch than stated in the pattern, use needles one size larger, and if you have less stitches, use needles one size smaller. Test on these needles too until you get the correct tension.

THREADING WOOL.—If darning needle has a small eye, first insert a double length of sewing thread. Pass one end of the wool through the loop of the thread and pull back through the eye of the needle.

WOOL.—Store in a polythene bag to keep safe from moths. Also, the colour can be seen at a glance.

ZIPPERS.—Slide fasteners on knitted garments should be as small as possible as a heavy fastener on fine wool will drag the fabric.

Slip a spring clothes peg over the needle when you lay aside your knitting to prevent stitches from slipping off the point.

9

Running Repairs

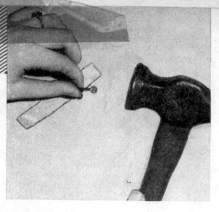

BUTTONS.—If these have lost their lustre, brighten by coating thinly with clear nail polish.

CASTERS.—After removing a broken caster, fill hole in foot of chair with plastic wood and allow to harden thoroughly before screwing in new caster.

DARK CLOTHING.—To remove fluff, use a dry sponge instead of a clothes brush.

FIREBACK.—If this has cracked and crumbled, remove loose pieces and brush out dirt and dust. Then pack crack with putty fire cement. Leave to harden before lighting fire.

GOLD.—Clean by washing in a soapy lather of lukewarm water. Dry with a cotton duster and polish vigorously with chamois leather.

GLUE.—Use a drawing-pin to re-seal the end of a tube of glue after use. This is better than an ordinary pin, for the wide flat head makes it easier to grip.

MARCASITE.—Bring back the sparkle to marcasite jewellery by running a stick of ordinary chalk lightly over the stones. Polish with a dry toothbrush and finish with a gentle rub with a soft, dry cloth.

METAL HANDLES.—If these work loose, refix securely with the plastic steel now available for the purpose.

NAILS.—If small and the hammer is large, use eyebrow tweezers to grip the nail firmly. This is particularly useful when replacing the backs of pictures.

PAILS OR CANS.—Repair metal or plastic pails which leak with the glass fibre kit sold for the purpose. The filler sets solid within half an hour.

PAINT.—After painting, put some of the left-over paint into an old nail varnish bottle with a fitted brush. This can be used to touch up any chips or scratches.

PATENT LEATHER.—A rub with a cloth dipped in cold milk will remove fingermarks.

PATENT LEATHER SHOES.—Preserve by occasionally rubbing in some pure olive oil with a flannel. Leave for a while, then polish with a dry cloth.

PEARLS.—If artificial pearl necklaces and ear-rings have lost their lustre, give them a coat of colourless nail varnish.

PLASTIC BATHS AND SINKS.—Treat scratches with a good metal polish, rubbing well in.

POTTERY.—When cracks appear in vases or ornaments, cover the cracks with china cement or, if the crack is tiny, try painting with two coats of gloss paint.

POLYTHENE BOWL.—Mend small holes by using a moderately hot iron and smoothing surrounding polythene inwards until hole is filled in.

PRAM HOOD.—Apply patch to inside, using fabric adhesive, and press the two edges of slit as closely together as possible over patch. Adhesive carpet tape can also be used.

SUEDE SHOES.—If these have become shiny, hold in the steam from a boiling kettle. Brush with a rubber or wire brush, then leave to let the moisture dry out.

TOWELS.—Strengthen thin places with rows of machining. Bind frayed edges with bias binding.

To avoid cracking plaster when driving in a nail, paste a piece of adhesive paper on the wall and drive the nail through this.

UMBRELLAS.—Rub a little petroleum jelly on the ribs and hinges of an umbrella occasionally. This will keep them smooth-running and rust-free.

ZIPP FASTENERS.—If a frock zipper tends to unfasten, sew a dress hook above it, then slip the tab opening of the zipp over the hook.

PLANTS

To test if a plant requires water, put a knitting needle into the soil. If no earth adheres to it, water immediately.

FEEDING.—Use a good liquid fertiliser regularly, following instructions for correct dose.

FROST.—Protect plants by keeping away from windows in autumn and winter.

TO KEEP.—During any absence from home, water each plant well before you leave. Slip pot into polythene bag and fasten with a rubber band. Move away from windows.

RE-POTTING.—Never do this in winter. Wait until spring or early summer, towards the end of the plant's resting season when new shoots are beginning to form.

To test whether or not to re-pot, put fingers over base of plant, invert pot and give it a sharp tap. The earth should come away cleanly, and you can determine if the roots are overcrowded and require more living room.

Allow at least an inch of flower-pot chips for drainage at base of new pot.

SOIL.—Keep this raked, and sponge any dust off leaves gently, as plants breathe through their leaves. In keeping foliage free from dust, a scent spray is useful. Fill with water and spray plants once a week.

WATERING.—Do not over-water, especially in winter. This is more harmful than under-watering. Keep a few bottles of water in a warm place for watering. Avoid using cold water from the tap.

Sewing Sense

BUTTONS.—When sewing buttons to coats or suits, slip a match between button and material. When match is slipped out it leaves a generous stem for the thread to be wound round before finishing off.

To remove a button safely, slide a comb underneath and cut the thread with a razor blade.

BUTTONHOLES.—Mark each place where you wish to make a buttonhole with clear nail varnish first. Allow to dry, then cut through the centre and the edges of the material will not fray so easily.

CUTTING OUT.—To make sure the material is on the straight, pick up a thread with a pin and draw it out. A clearly visible line will be left as a guide.

CUTTING OUT.—Lay the paper pattern on the material and, instead of pinning, press lightly with a hot iron. The pattern then clings to the material, making the cutting easier.

and FLOWERS

BEFORE ARRANGING.—Strip off all lower leaves and stand in deep water in a dark place for at least an hour—overnight is better. This hardens them and fills the stems with water.

Fill the vase with warm water before putting in the flowers. Keep heads of short-stemmed flowers near the water.

FOLIAGE.—Soak in a bath of water overnight before arranging.

HOLLOW STEMS.—Turn flowers upside down and fill the stems with water. Place a finger over the opening, and only release it when the stems are under water in the vase.

POPPIES.—Seal these and all other flowers with milky sap in their stems by holding them in a candle flame for a few seconds.

TULIPS AND IRISES.—Cut the white part from the lower stems to make them last longer. This part is fibrous and prevents the water from reaching the blooms.

WOODY STEMS.—Crush or split the stems before putting into water.

TO REVIVE.—Treat drooping flowers by wrapping newspaper tightly round each stem. Leave up to the heads in water overnight.

WATER.—Keep a tablet of charcoal in the water and this will keep it pure much longer.

Revive drooping flowers by wrapping stems tightly in newspaper, and leave up to head in water overnight.

EMBROIDERY THREADS.—Prevent tangling once the skein is broken by pushing the two paper bands round them into the centre till they meet.

GATHERING.—When making gathering stitches use a nylon thread as this is stronger and has more "give."

HOLDERS.—For pins and needles use old fountain pen cases as holders. They can be clipped on to the side of your work basket.

MARKING FABRICS.—Instead of using tailor's chalk for marking notches, hems and buttonholes, use a nail white pencil. This does not rub off so easily.

NEEDLES.—When you have finished sewing don't stick your needle through the cotton on the reel as this splits the thread. Instead, stuff the centre hole of the reel with cotton wool and push the needle into that.

NOTCHES.—When cutting notches, cut the V with the point outwards. This prevents you cutting too far in and spoiling the seam.

NYLONS.—When repairing nylon stockings, wear a black glove on the hand you slip into the stocking. You'll see the ladder more clearly.

PAPER PATTERNS.—When a dress pattern becomes so wrinkled that it is difficult to work with, place it under wax paper and smooth with a cool iron.

Check your measurements against the pattern pieces. If the bodice is too long make a fold in the pattern. To lengthen, cut along guiding line given on pattern and insert a strip of paper.

REELS.—Keep your sewing reels neat and tidy by sliding them on to a long knitting needle. Fix a small cork over the pointed end to keep them in place.

SCISSORS.—After use, stick the points into a cork.

SEAMS.—Before ripping seams with a knife or razor, wrap the blade with adhesive tape to within one inch of the end. This helps to prevent injury to the fingers.

SEAM PRESSING.—When dressmaking, every dart and seam should be pressed as you go along. It is a good idea to set up your ironing board beside your sewing machine before you start.

SEATED SKIRT.—Place on table with seated part in centre. Cover with a damp cloth, then iron in small circles with a moderately hot iron, holding the weight of the iron in the hand. Press as usual.

TAPE MEASURE.—To renew crispness, iron under a sheet of waxed paper, making sure that the iron is not too hot.

TWEED SKIRTS.—If these have gone limp after washing, add two tablespoonfuls of painter's size to the final rinsing water to restore firmness.

Home Truths

GLASSES.—Use paper tissues for polishing glasses and cutlery. There is no fluff, and the articles are left shining clean.

GLASS STOPPER.—When a glass stopper is stuck fast, pour a little glycerine round the neck and let it stand until the stopper comes out easily.

GRATER.—After grating cheese, vegetables and so on, finish off with a crust of dry bread. This will remove most of the sticky bits on the grater.

IVORY.—When ivory handles of cutlery become discoloured, rub with slices of lemon dipped in salt. Rinse with warm water and dry thoroughly.

JELLY PANS.—After use fill with warm water and leave to soak. Wash with hot water. If badly stained, use vinegar and salt, rinsing again straight away.

Before using oven glassware, rub well with onion. This helps to prevent cracking.

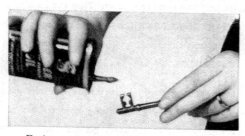

Easiest way to oil a keyhole is to put the oil on the key and turn this in the lock until the action eases.

KITCHEN GADGETS.—When an egg whisk, mincer or other gadget becomes stiff and difficult to work, put a few drops of glycerine on the working parts.

KEYS.—If new keys are too sharp, smooth them by folding a piece of emery paper and rubbing the cut edge of the key along the fold of the paper.

LINEN.—To distinguish linen from cotton, place a drop of glycerine on the material. On linen it is quickly absorbed and forms a transparent spot, but on cotton it is not absorbed and rolls up like a drop of mercury.

MIRRORS.—To prevent clouding, rub with cloth wrung out in hot water and sprinkled with glycerine. Polish mirrors and glass with old nylon stockings, as these leave no streaks on the surface.

NAILS.—To make them hold better and resist rust, coat well with nail polish and leave until thoroughly dry before using.

PILLOWSLIPS. — When worn, mend by covering the thin part with a pretty handkerchief. Pin on diagonally and stitch.

PICTURES.—To keep a picture straight on the wall, glue a strip of sandpaper to the bottom of the frame at the back.
Clean the glass covering pictures with a cloth dampened with methylated spirits.
To prevent picture frames streaking the wall, press a drawing-pin into the lower edge of the frame at the back of the picture.

PLAYING CARDS.—Clean with a piece of cotton wool soaked in milk or apply a little white furniture cream on a soft cloth; leave for a few minutes; then polish carefully with a clean cloth.

PLASTIC SINK PROTECTOR.—To make this fit, heat gently until slightly pliable, then mould by pressing over the sink edge. When firm again it will remain in place.

SCISSORS.—Tighten loose scissors by heating a poker and holding it to each side of the rivet for a few minutes, then give both sides a tap with a hammer.

SCREW-TOP JARS.—If the top is stiff, twist an elastic band two or three times round the lid to give you a good grip.

SHOE POLISH.—When polish has gone hard and lumpy, pour in a little vinegar and leave to soak for about an hour.

SILVERWARE.—Pieces of silver which are not used often should be wrapped separately in soft tissue paper then placed in Polythene bags.

SOAP.—Press the metal cap from a lemonade bottle into a new cake of soap to form a stand and prevent wastage.

SOAP SCRAPS.—Put into a saucepan with a little cold water; heat gently until a clear liquid; then pour into old patty tins and leave to set.

SPECTACLES.—Use eau-de-cologne to clean spectacles. It quickly removes spots and grease from lenses and keeps them from steaming up.

STRING HOLDER.—Put a ball of string inside an old teapot and let the string come out of the spout.

TUMBLERS.—If two stick together, fill the inside one with cold water, then place both in a basin of hot water, and they should separate quite easily.

VACUUM FLASKS.—Freshen by filling three-quarters full of warm water and adding one teaspoonful of baking soda. Replace the stopper and shake vigorously. Rinse with warm water.

WASH LEATHER.—Before using for the first time, put half a teaspoonful of vinegar in water and soak leather in this for a time to make it soft and pliable.

Printed and Published in Great Britain by
John Leng & Co., Ltd., and D. C. Thomson & Co., Ltd., Dundee, Glasgow, Manchester and London.

The Wonderful Language OF Flowers

It is important to know what flowers mean when giving or receiving them. Flowers have wonderful meanings. In Victorian days, flowers were used as a way to express feelings and to communicate them. If the sender had something in mind that the recipient was not aware of, or the recipient was more conscious of the meanings than the gentle sender, chaos could ensue, or hearts could be broken - such is the importance of The Language of Flowers.

Here is a listing of different flowers with their meanings - some old fashioned - some you can't get so easily these days, but fascinating nevertheless, collected over many years :-

A

Acacia - Very secret love
Acorn - A Nordic symbol of life and immortality
Aloe - Sadness, grief
Allspice - Compassion
Ambrosia - Love returned.
Amaryllis - Pride, timidity
Anemone - Unfading or undying love
Angelica - Inspiration
Aniseed - The restoration of youth
Arbutis - Only love - one love
Apple - Preference
Aspidistra - The last thing on the stall, but I love you.
Aster - Love; daintiness; lightness
Azalea - Take care of yourself (for me); a fragile passion

Azalea

B
Bachelor Button - Celibacy
Baby's Breath - Everlasting, unfailing love
Basil - Very Best Wishes, love
Bay Leaf - Strength
Begonia - Beware; be careful
Bells Of Ireland - Good luck
Bird Of Paradise - Magnificence
Bittersweet - Truth
Bluebell - Humility; constancy
Borage - Courage
Bouquet of withered flowers - Rejection; rejected love
Burnet - A merry and gay heart
Buttercup - Cheerfulness

Bay leaf

C
Cactus - Endurance; warmth
Calendula - Sheer joy
Camellia - Admiration; perfection; a good luck gift to a man
Candytuft - Indifference
Carnation - Bonds of affection; health; energy; fascination
Carnation (pink) - I will never forget you
Carnation (purple) - Capriciousness; whimsicality
Carnation (red) - An aching heart ; admiration
Carnation (single, solid color) - Yes !
Carnation (striped)- No; a refusal; I can't come to you
Carnation (white) - Sweet ; innocent; pure love; a woman's good luck gift
Carnation (yellow) - Rejection; utter disdain
Cattail - Peace; prosperity ; wealth
Camomile - Patience; attracts wealth
Chrysanthemum (in general) - Cheerfulness; you are the most wonderful friend
Chrysanthemum (red) - Love
Chrysanthemum (white) - Truth
Chrysanthemum (yellow) - Slighted love
Coriander - Lust
Cowslip - Pensiveness; winning grace
Crocus - Cheerfulness; abuse me not
Cyclamen - Resignation and goodbye
Clover - Good luck

Clover

Eucalyptus

D

Daffodil - Respect
Daisy - Innocence
Dandelion - May your wishes come true

E

Eucalyptus - Protection

Fennel

F

Fennel - Worthy of all praise
Fern - Sincerity
Forget-Me-Not - True love
Fern (Magic) - Fascination; confidence and shelter
Fern (Maidenhair) - A secret bond of love
Feverfew - Protection
Fir - Time
Flax - Domestic symbol; fate
Forget-me-not - True love; memories
Forsythia - Anticipation

G

Gardenia - You are lovely; my secret love
Garland of roses - A reward of virtue
Garlic - Courage; strength
Geranium (Scented) - Preference
Gladiolus - Love at first sight
Grass - Submission

Forget=Me=Not

Grass cuttings - I've cut the grass - come for a picnic
Heather (lavender) - Admiration; solitude
Heather (white) - Protection; Your wishes will come true

H

Heather - Welcome (to Bonnie Scotland)
Hibiscus - Delicate beauty
Holly - Good will, defence; domestic bliss ; foresight
Honeysuckle - Generous and devoted affection
Hyacinth (general) - Games and sports; rashness;
flower dedicated to Apollo
Hyacinth (blue) - Constancy

218

Hyacinth (purple) - I am sorry; please forgive me; sorrow
Hyacinth (red or pink) - Play
Hyacinth (white) - Loveliness
Hyacinth (yellow) - Jealousy
Hydrangea - Thank you for understanding; frigidity; heartlessness
Hyssop - Wards away evil spirits

Iris - Faith; hope; wisdom and valour
Ivy - Fidelity and friendship
Ivy - A sprig of white tendrils - Anxious to please; fond affection

Jasmine

Japanese Knotweed - stay away; don't become entangled with me
Jasmine - Amiability; attracts wealth
Jonquil - Love me; affection returned; desire; sympathy;
    strong desire for a return of affection
Juniper - Protection

Larkspur - Fickleness
Lavender - Absolute devotion
Lemon - Zest
Lemon Balm - Brings love
Lemon verbena - Attracts opposite sex
Lily (general) - Keeps unwanted callers
    or visitors away
Lily (calia) - Beauty

Lily (day) - Coquetry
Lily (eucharis) - Maiden charms
Lily (orange) - Hatred
Lily (tiger) - Wealth; pride
Lily (white) - Virginity; purity; majesty; it is wonderful
  to be with you
Lily (yellow) - I'm walking on air
Lily of the valley - sweetness; a return to happiness;
  humility

Magnolia - Sweetness; beauty; love of nature

Lily

Marigold - Comforts the heart
Mint - Protection from illness; warmth of feeling
Marjoram (sweet) - Joy and happiness
Mistletoe - Kiss me; affection; to surmount difficulties; sacred plant of India
Monkshood - Beware, an enemy is near; chivalry
Moss - Maternal love; charity
Myrtle - Love; A Hebrew emblem of marriage

Marigold

Narcissus - Egotism; formality; stay as sweet as you are
Nasturtium - Conquest; victory in battle; maternal love; charity; patriotism

Nettles - Beware of sharp jaggies and enemies

Oleander - Caution; beware
Orange - Generosity
Orange Blossom - Wisdom
Orchid - Love; beauty; refinement; beautiful lady; the Chinese symbol for many children
Orchid (cattleya)

Mature charm

Palm leaves - Victory and success
Pansy - Thoughts; love
Peach - Longevity
Peony - An aphrodisiac
Petunia - Resentment; anger; your presence calms me
Pine - Hope; pity
Poppy (general) - Eternal sleep ; oblivion; imagination
Poppy (red) - Pleasure; consolation

Pink Orchids

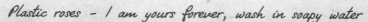

Plastic roses - I am yours forever, wash in soapy water

220

Poppy (white) - Consolation; sleep
Poppy (yellow) - Wealth; success
Prickly Pear - Satire
Primrose - I can't go on without you; early youth
Primrose (evening) - Inconstancy

 Rose(general)(Red) - Love ; I love you
Rose(white) - Eternal Love; innocence; heavenly; secrecy and silence
Rose(pink) - Perfect happiness; please believe me

Rose (Yellow) - Friendship ; jealousy; try to care
Rose (Black) -Death
Rose (red and white) - Togetherness ; unity
Rose (thornless) - Love at first sight
Rose (single, full bloom) - I love you; I still love you; I really do
Rose bud - Beauty and youth; a heart innocent of love
Rose bud (red) - Pure and lovely
Rose bud (white) - Girlhood
Rose bud (moss) - Confessions of love
Roses (Bouquet of full bloom) - Gratitude
Roses (Garland or crown of) - Beware of virtue; reward of merit; crown ; a symbol of superior merit
Roses (musk cluster) - Charming
Rose (tea) - I'll always remember you / us / our time together
Rose (cabbage) - Ambassador of love
Rose (Christmas) - Tranquilise my anxiety; anxiety
Rose (damask) - Brilliant complexion
Rose (dark crimson) - Mourning
Rose (hibiscus) - Delicate beauty
Rose leaf - You may hope
Rosemary - Remembrance

Poppy

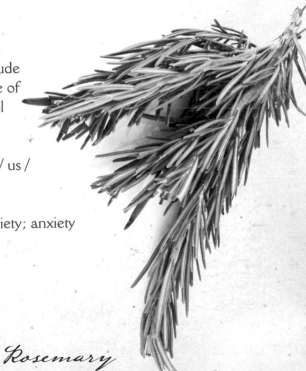

Rosemary

Sage Wisdom - I wish you long life
Salvia (blue) - Thinking of you
Smilax - Loveliness
Snapdragon - Deception; gracious lady; presumption
Snowdrop - Hope and warmth
Spiderflower - Elope with me
Stephanotis - Happiness in marriage; desire to travel
Stock - Lasting beauty
Strawberry - Perfect goodness
Sunflower - Loyalty; wishes
Sweetpea - Goodbye; departure; blissful pleasure; Thank you for a lovely time

Snowdrops

Thyme - Strength and courage; ensures restful sleep
Tulip (general) - Fame,charity; perfect lover
Tulip (red) - Believe me; declaration of love
Tulip (variegated) - Beautiful eyes
Tulip (yellow) - Hopeless love

Thyme

Thistle (Or any one of the genera Cnicus, Craduus, and Onopordon) - Prickly

Violet - Modesty; calms tempers; induces sleep
Violet (blue) - Watchfulness; faithfulness; I'll always be true
Violet (white) - Let's take a chance on happiness
Viscaria - Will you dance with me?

Violets

Woodruff - sweet humility

Yarrow

Yarrow - Health, healing

Zinnia - Thoughts of friends
Zinnia (magenta) - Lasting affection
Zinnia (mixed) - Thinking of an absent friend
Zinnia (scarlet) - Constancy

Zinnia